UNDERSTANDING THE ALPHA CHILD AT HOME AND SCHOOL

Alpha children are often stigmatized by labels of learning disability, emotional disturbance or other sorts of behavior incompetencies. However, the authors point out that children who have unusual response styles should be seen as normal children in their own right. With the realization of unequalized hemispheric capacities, extensive changes in the basic foundations of educational philosophy and structure are needed. The approaches outlined here offer both teacher and parent new methods which will help to meet the needs of the alpha child.

UNDERSTANDING
THE ALPHA CHILD
AT HOME AND SCHOOL

UNDERSTANDING THE ALPHA CHILD AT HOME AND SCHOOL

LEFT AND RIGHT HEMISPHERIC FUNCTION IN RELATION TO PERSONALITY AND LEARNING

By

JACK L. FADELY, Ed.D.

*Associate Professor of Special Education
and Educational Psychology
Butler University, College of Education
Indianapolis, Indiana*

and

VIRGINIA N. HOSLER, M.S.

*Diagnostic Learning Center
Peoria Public Schools
Peoria, Illinois*

Illustrations By

Debbie Frank

CHARLES C THOMAS • PUBLISHER
Springfield • Illinois • U.S.A.

Published and Distributed Throughout the World by
CHARLES C THOMAS • PUBLISHER
Bannerstone House
301-327 East Lawrence Avenue, Springfield, Illinois, U.S.A.

© *1979, by* CHARLES C THOMAS • PUBLISHER
ISBN 0-398-03862-7
Library of Congress Catalog Card Number: 78-24687

Printed in the United States of America
V-R-1

Library of Congress Cataloging in Publication Data
Fadely, Jack L., et al.
    Understanding the alpha child at home
and school.

    Bibliography: p. 229
    Includes index.
    78-24687
    ISBN 0-398-03862-7

PREFACE

THE discussion in this book attempts to give the teacher and educational psychologist a new viewpoint concerning learning, personality, and child development. The authors do not intend that this work should be accepted as a definitive outline of a holistic theory which can drastically alter much of the present methodology in learning and development. Much of what has been discussed is still at the theory development phase. Yet, for too long psychologists and educators have attempted to understand and even definitively describe child development from an inferential viewpoint utilizing tests and concepts which are too constrictive to meet the needs of the problems children present in both learning and behavior. It is the author's hope that this book, with its many implications, will provide a base for new directions in learning.

That there is a generalized tendency toward lateralization in brain function into the left and right hemispheres is not doubted. The full implication of that lateralization is yet to be substantially demonstrated in the process of meeting the needs of children. Exactly how various developmental neuro-functions and environment interact to produce the complex and varied behaviors of individual children is still a problem which will confront us each time a different child is met in the classroom. The human mind, like a computer, must be programmed. The potential possibilities in learning and behavior are too great for a single practitioner to comprehend. The human mind, again not unlike the computer, is fond of producing definition for data fed into it. The research strongly suggests that in the normally developed human being, the left hemisphere is the locus of mind control which organizes such data. Yet, the role of the various other neurological areas within the central nervous system dealing with cognitive function is less than clear and certainly more complex than the simple notion of a singular hemisphere.

The role of the right hemisphere, production of creative thought in spatial integration and in nonverbal intelligence, is a new horizon for psychology and education. The realization that cerebral dominance can be manifested not only in motor dominance and language but, as in the case of the right hemisphere, in a totally different form of thought has implications that should alert the professional to new possibilities in behavior. To know that there are children and adults who function from somewhat a dominant nonverbal cognitive process as opposed to the conventional language-based process must turn our attention to new ways of looking at both learning and behavior.

In many respects this discussion about the Alpha children, the naturalized children, is not new. It is just that now what has always been known can be reevaluated from the standpoint of normal behavior instead of a learning disability, emotional disturbance, or other sorts of behavioral incompetencies. Children who have unusual response styles may be seen as normal children in their own right, individuals who, in their unique way, have as much right to be accepted for what they are as the typical left-minded and language-dominated individual.

Accepting the imagination, the creativity, and the differing viewpoint in perception and learning of the right hemispheric dominant individual will provide the opportunity to learn how to teach him, how to assist him in adjusting in a language-oriented culture, and provide for him a meaningful place in society. When compared to the usual language-oriented child in the past, the creative and holistic child has been seen as abnormal and the subject of "treatment" to make him like everyone else. In the process it is staggering to consider how many capable children have been made into hopeless neurotics because they too finally assumed that they were in some way deviant.

The natural child with normal verbal intelligence can learn to live in the usual way. He can be taught all of the skills and behaviors of anyone else. But he has to be taught differently, accepted for his differences, and encouraged to learn. The Alpha child is the child who, for genetic or environmental reasons, has adopted a predominantly nonverbal style of life while the other extreme, the uncreative and dogmatic Theta child, is bound to convention, to order and logic, and to adhering closely to accepted models of life-styles. In between are those people who might be considered most appropriately "normal," those individuals who display equalized competencies in both hemispheres with adequate integration of both forms of thought. But the possible combinations and shadings of children for either form of thought are endless, making an accurate diagnosis difficult. However, this is exactly the importance of the naturalized-socialized dichotomy: giving value to both forms of behavior provides for an extension, an enlargement of understanding human behavior in all of its complexities. It allows the teachers and the psychologists to finally go beyond the concept of good and bad, well and sick, intact or disabled. It allows us to look at behavior and learning potential without the need to treat or make well all individuals who happen to differ from the usual child. It is this possibility that will make working with children in this stance most difficult, for the typical teacher and psychologist need compact, well-defined limits and directions. This has been the root of our difficulty. Human beings are not linear. They are multi-dimensional. Most conventional, language-based thought is founded on linear and deductive thought, not multi-leveled possibilities and variables. Using linear thought, the naturalized child can be thought out of existence simply by failing to see behavior in the complex and multi-faced way in which it truly occurs.

In final analysis the authors have found, in their work with children, adolescents, and adults, that while the endless specifics of the naturalized-socialized theory will continue to involve constant research and refinement, the neurological validation is not so important as the many approaches which are available through application of the theory. It is a theory of behavior and behavior potentials which is at least tentatively founded in concepts of neurology.

If there is a major drawback of this book it is that it is too brief to clearly outline all of the possibilities and potentialities involved in the theory presented. Yet, there is little doubt that the complexities and implications of the work presented require careful and rigorous study by the reader introduced for the first time to such concepts. The references given in many sections of the book will provide additional material for anyone wishing to read more, but much of the book is free from the usual documentation — which often lends authenticity as well as careful structure, rendering even the strongest of the naturalized thinkers bored and overwhelmed with justifications and rationalizations. The authors continue their work with children and as others, will continue to document, to expose repeated experimentation, and to continue to question all that has been said here. Work with brain lateralization theory is already forming a new frontier of behavioral research throughout the country and the coming years should see much development.

The final word is of the sadness that is already developing around the lateralization theory throughout the literature. Many popular articles are appearing and most repeat what such researchers as Ornstein and Sperry have already said. These researchers are involved primarily in a noneducational effort. They do not work with children every day in the classroom. Those writers who attempt to translate their work in a simplistic way into education are already developing a following of "new frontiers," disciples who run the risk of inciting another national movement such as learning disabilities or dyslexia, simple labels applied wholesale to millions of children. Such movements do little to help either the child or the teacher. It is hoped that this book may in some small way lend braking effects to such movements so that we can all learn as we go in small steps and not look for another false panacea for our problems.

INTRODUCTION

THE field of education has come a long way since Thomas Dewey first advocated his concept of "progressive education." Psychological theory has advanced beyond Freud's basic constructs of human personality, and the culture has realized profound changes in both technologies and life-styles since the turn of the century. In recent years, parents and teachers have become exposed to a host of advanced ideas, theories, and assumptions concerning how children develop and how they learn. Few professionals in the general fields of education and psychology have been able to keep abreast of even a minor part of the information generated by research in development and learning. The only professionals who maintain a balanced perspective are those who continue to work with children in the school and community setting. This daily involvement, along with extensive reading, make it possible to become immersed in the relevant issues and changes currently appearing in the culture.

This book is intended to suggest that, even though much has been learned about children and the process of educational achievement, about the sequence and nature of developmental abilities, and about the complex issues in socialization during childhood, there is a ghost in the machine. Still another great drama is currently emerging within the study of human personality which will drastically alter even the more recent and fast-paced changes in our understanding of human behavior.

The most recent discovery in human behavior has been the tentative findings of a broad range of researchers concerning neurological differences between the left and right cerebral hemispheres. These differences in basic functions of the two hemispheres not only seem to affect learning, but also behavior in some surprising ways. It appears that each hemisphere of the brain, while quite similar in neuro-structure, does demonstrate differences in total mass and weight, as well as in significant integrative functions. Each hemisphere is able to receive and recognize the same sort of sensory information such as sound, vision, smell, tactile, and kinesthetic data. Yet, while each hemisphere is able to receive the same information, this information is processed differently relative to the hemisphere's particular mode of organization. While genetic structure predetermines the nature of the hemisphere's tendency to process information in a specific manner, the neuro-structure has to *learn* its unique functions and organization.

The right hemisphere seems to involve a range of nonverbal integrative functions including holistic perception, space and form perception, directional orientation visual imagery, and other such activity. The left hemisphere appears to be "pre-wired" genetically to organize language, to store language information, to learn values, and to provide the seat of socialization capabilities. This differential and specialized integrative capacity of each hemisphere provides the basis for a seeming duality of being and awareness in each of us which is usually synthesized into one consciousness, a unified feeling of being, and a complete temporal-spatial structure of perception and learning. Is this truly the case?

The implications of this question are important for learning. Do we tend to oversocialize the child by stimulating left hemispheric or language development while minimizing and neglecting the right hemispheric or natural spatial-motoric aspects of our being? Are there effects of equalized competencies in the two hemispheres? Is it possible that unequal capabilities tend to produce a child with special personality and learning styles? Are there effects on the development of such skills as reading, writing, spelling, or math as a consequence of uneven or unequal development in one hemisphere over the other? The answers to these questions appear to be affirmative, which could require extensive changes in the basic foundations of educational philosophy and structure.

Many professionals suggest that even Freud's concept of the Ego, Superego, and Id may be correlated to specific functions of the left or right hemisphere. It may be that the Ego involves a collective personal awareness of spatial-temporal information in both hemispheres. Superego may involve specialized information which relates to social values and is primarily stored in the left hemisphere. The Id, or seat of the libido drive energy, may arise from the naturalistic and unsocialized right hemisphere. The integration of personality concepts with neurological organization could be a significant development in bringing the whole issue of consciousness and unconsciousness into the light of observable understanding for the first time.

This book is concerned with the effects of unequalized hemispheric capacities. The most important issue for the parent and teacher may be the existence of normal children who develop learning styles and personality structures which are not organized in the traditional manner but in ways which make it difficult for the child to adapt his behavior to the conventional system of behavior and learning. These children are called the Alpha children for they are special children who are "normal" in their own way and yet are seen as abnormal in a society which is organized in a different manner.

These writers' research and work with children and adolescents has continually led to assumptions which often did not seem to have any adequate explanation relative to established theories of personality and child development. Many of the children and adolescents exhibited certain behavioral and learning characteristics which suggest a peculiar and yet obvious syndrome of central nervous system function. A review of the research in neurology and psychoneurology has since convinced us that there is another and often overlooked way of explaining particular sets of learning and behavioral problems of children and adolescents which, though obvious in diagnostic situations, is often overlooked because the diagnostician has no theory or assumption that might lead him to recognize the particular cluster of factors.

The theory which we have slowly developed is tentative at best; extensive study must continue if we are to be able to eventually use the cluster of characteristics surrounding Alpha children to benefit teachers and parents in assisting these individuals in their general development and learning processes. The discussions in the following chapters are presented for empirical testing by psychologists, teachers, and parents in school settings. Such involvement should bring to light more clearly the specific nature of the processes involved. Enough experience is available to suggest many approaches and methods which may be used with these children both in parental management of their behavior at home and in teacher supervision of learning techniques at school. These approaches are outlined in this book so that both the teacher and parent may attempt to meet the needs of these children. However, it should be remembered that the process we are dealing with is yet to be fully clarified or understood, and therefore the adult will need to proceed cautiously, comparing notes with other professionals who may be involved with the child.

Their major tasks will be learning more about the Alpha child and developing alternate methods of teaching him. Alpha children become Alpha adults and, as we engage the attention of such children, we may learn as much about ourselves as about the children.

ACKNOWLEDGMENTS

WE express our appreciation to all who have assisted in the preparation of this book. In particular, we wish to acknowledge Dr. John M. McLean of Neurological Associates in Peoria, Illinois for his helpful recommendations for modifying the research presentation in the text. We also wish to thank Sonna Aden for her patience and assistance in editing the text and Debbie Frank for the drawings. Sharon Dorsey was helpful in her assistance with the typing. From countless sources have come ideas and suggestions that find their expression in this book.

J.L.F.
V.N.H.

CONTENTS

Chapter 1

THE NATURAL CHILD

CHILDHOOD comes quietly like spring winds blowing softly from the south, impatient to see the dawning of today. The young child runs unchained through his early years looking for surprises. His is a new world never seen before. He touches, tastes, listens, and watches every movement about him as he learns. He explores endlessly and measures each hour carefully upon the scale of experience gained yesterday. He accumulates experience and restlessly waits for more. This is the natural child. The natural child is curious and loves life for what it causes him to feel and how it teaches him mastery of both himself and the world about him. Childhood is a time when one can be enthusiastic simply because something is learned. Learning to walk, to finally climb the stairs alone, to predict how things will behave, and to tell about experiences are all ends in themselves and give the child ever growing confidence and determination to continue to explore.

But something intervenes in this happy, reckless race of natural behavior that is part of the heritage of every child the world over. Socialization begins at birth, and for most children the struggle to simply "be" is slowly lost as he learns "how" he ought to be. The struggle ends sometime about the sixth year for most children as their unbounded curiosity and enthusiasm is directed into socially appropriate behavior and toward values which will shape them into acceptable human beings ready for school and the responsibilities of belonging to groups. Becoming a responsible human being who participates effectively in society is important to all of us. Socialization, as Freud and others postulated, is one of the major tasks of becoming an adjusted human being. Left to our childhood dreams, most of us would make poor leaders and members of an integrated culture which provides the comforts and security of the usual world. But there is a bit of desire in all of our inner beings to be free, to take flight on our fantasies, and be whatever pleases us.

If we simply think for a moment, we may realize that early childhood was the most natural part of our lives. It was in those early years that we had unbounded enthusiasm and desire to know, to feel, to see, and experience whatever delighted our senses. That desire grows out of a most important part of the naturalness in each of us. The young child sees his world from an experiential point of view. He does not know yet how to evaluate experience as good or bad, but regards it simply as relative to how it makes him feel. Such a pleasure, to simply know the moment, to experience it — fully drinking in every sensation! Who can forget the moment late in the evening when mother pulled the blanket up over us and kissed us goodnight? We cannot forget the fondness we felt when someone held us close, the pleasure at the taste of strawberry ice cream, or the thrill of riding that first roller coaster in the spring of our lives. Wonderful impressions of what has held meaning for us are stored in our memories and we cling to them hoping for yet many more to come. If we stop for a moment to consider these memories, a curious thought comes to mind. Most of these memories involve things we felt, tasted, touched, or sensed in the most basic way. When we remember a favorite poem, it is not so much the words we recall as the images which the words represent. Feelings return along with the images and pictures which are recalled. Much of our memory is based on the ability to recall images of places and situations. The words used to stimulate memory appear to act as a sort of neat and orderly filing system which can locate the images and feelings necessary for recall.

The Formation of Consciousness

The parent or teacher who is given the task of assisting children grow into well-adjusted and competent adults has an awesome task. Perhaps one of the most significant personal benefits of watching and teaching children is what we learn about ourselves through the lives of children. When we observe and work with young children, much of our own beginning is recalled and becomes more clearly understood. The adult learns how he experienced his early years, and often such insight changes his concept of himself. Understanding children requires that the adult engage in much self-evaluation and reflection in order to have empathy and insight into the needs of children. But just observing is often not enough. Each adult usually desires to give the child as much advantage in his struggle into adulthood as possible, perhaps more than he may have experienced in his own childhood. Somehow working with children also gives the adult a second chance to experience his own childhood in a different way.

One of the most significant early developmental milestones of childhood is the growing self-awareness and consciousness which comes to be the personality perceived by others. During the first few weeks of life, the infant merely responds to his environment both with initial reflex behaviors and with more complex perceptual awareness. Infants come into life with much more than was once thought. There is significant ability to comprehend space and depth, and to discriminate between various shapes, forms, and even color or shadings.

The young infant is busy, during those first few weeks and months, perceiving and storing images, sounds, feelings, tactile experience, and gaining practice in controlling his own movements and responses. It is difficult to say when he actually becomes aware of himself, conscious of his being, and aware of his own existence as an entity separate from all of the stimuli about him. The developmental tasks ahead are awesome and the first year is a period of unbelievable growth and maturation. About the end of the first year, the infant is ready to begin learning words and to make some sense out of the sounds he has been hearing all about him. There has always been much discussion and argument about when the infant begins to learn language and about whether he is genetically programmed for language learning or whether he learns it through culture and experience. Recent research suggests that much of the facility for language is present even in the two-week-old infant. It has been enlightening to find the variety of perceptual capabilities which are present early in infancy.

Using an analysis of brain wave activity, it is possible to determine when particular parts of the brain are engaged in some sort of activity, when at rest but aware, and when in a state normally assigned as sleep. This analysis is possible by an electroencephalogram (EEG) which involves placing electrodes on various positions of the scalp and recording the minute electrical activity occurring in a specific area of the brain. Different patterns of brain wave activity are known to represent various states of mental activity, alertness, or inactivity. Through this sort of study it has been found that when infants hear sounds that contain phonetic structure, the left hemisphere of the brain becomes active while the right appears to be at rest. Conversely when nonlanguage sounds are provided the right hemisphere becomes active with the left becoming inactive. This research has been done with infants suggesting that, as early as two weeks, the brain is already performing differentially.

Such research raises the distinct possibility that the infant comes into the world with an already existent neurological structure which is predisposed to processing language units. Such research has also raised the probability that the two hemispheres of the brain, while receiving the same information, apparently react differently. Spatial information dealing with shape, size, color, depth, and a host of other nonlanguage information appears to be the most utilized in the right hemisphere. This differential behavior of the two hemispheres is quite significant, and more attention will be given to it in the following discussions.

But what of consciousness? It is apparent that our earlier experiences are those dealing with spatial forms, shapes, movement of objects, and nonverbal activity in our environment since we do not have the sophistication to make language sense out of it. When the mother first holds and fondles her newborn infant it is the touch, the warmth, and the nurturing relationship which is perceived by the infant. In essence, much of what the child learns in his earliest experience is that which is nonverbal. The young infant responds and becomes aware of his surroundings and himself through touching, feeling, tasting, and through awareness of internal and external movement. There develops a predominantly nonverbal world of meaning for each of us during our first year of life. Interestingly enough, it appears that our most sensitive memories in adulthood are those which are nonverbal.

We become conscious of ourselves through feelings, through visual and auditory differentiation between what we are and what occurs inside of us. We can early distinguish between internal sensory information and that which is coming from external sources through an innate and basic neurological mechanism. In this silent world devoid of language, we listen and see but do not speak. Images come to us and we react to them with feelings of pleasure or pain, of surprise or recognition, of excitement or boredom, of curiosity or disinterest. So it is with the young child and with the adult who, at a most fundamental level of awareness, also lives in a private world in which language plays only a partial role.

All of us have experiences from which we draw meaning without language as a mediator. It is the right hemisphere, the "nonlanguage" hemisphere of the brain, which is used to recognize faces, interpret certain mannerisms and gestures, feel what another is feeling, and respond to tenderness or love without words. Try walking in the park and watch people without being close enough to hear the words. You will find that the world has nearly as much meaning without words as it does when we are actively conversing in usual language. We can see the happiness and surprise of young children playing, the cautious and loving glances between a man and woman. We are sensitive to individuals lost in meditation and thought which can be understood as painful, pleasurable, or problem-solving in nature — all from merely watching without hearing. If you can keep from talking to yourself, you will find that you are more acutely aware and sensitive to human behavior than you thought and all beyond the world of words. During such moments, if we could measure your brain waves, we would not be surprised to find that you are conscious primarily in the right hemisphere. Your consciousness at that moment is distinctly different than when you are thinking in words or listening to someone talk. You are aware at the most basic level of your being; you are thinking in naturalistic patterns which we call naturalized thought to distinguish it from language-based thinking or socialized consciousness. The child's earliest awareness of his being comes from this naturalistic mode of thinking in the right hemisphere, the silent and most aware and sensitive part of our being.

The natural child runs, plays, explores and experiences his sensory world, and is full of joy and curiosity. But this natural mode of being has many other characteristics. For example, the child does not learn "right" and "wrong" behavior until he learns language. When the child or the adult is engaged in natural thought, he responds only to pain and pleasure, love and tenderness, threat or security. He does not label it "right" or "wrong" until language values are learned. Language and values are the rope tossed about the neck of the racing stallion so that we can harness his flight, often confining his first and natural consciousness forever. As the young child learns language he learns socially acceptable behaviors.

The developing system of words and values are learned through left hemisphere development and training. As the child matures, left hemispheric processes become the primary concern of consciousness. One does not simply run about as a free being for there are certain ways that one should behave and respond to other individuals. As the child learns more and more, language conflicts can develop between his naturalistic tendencies and his developing social or language values. By the time a child is five years old he is well on his way to using language and social value structure as his primary mode of thinking and perceiving his world. Naturalistic thought gives way to logic, to time and values, to learning how to behave in acceptable ways in order to structure the world into meaningful relationships. Slowly, the child becomes less a child and more a developing adult. Finally, the naturalistic patterns of behavior are repressed in favor of language and social meaning.

Lateralization

The process of utilizing one or the other side of the brain for specialized functions is called lateralization. Specific functions of behavior and perception are developed in one lateral side of the brain or the other. This aspect of human behavior and development is most likely the key to our tremendous adaptive ability which far exceeds that of most animals even though some lateralization occurs in other animals. The specialization and lateralization of the brain provides for a mathematically magnificent organization in human beings. The two sides of the brain are quite similar in structure and size and are both capable of responding to visual, auditory, tactile, kinesthetic, and emotional information. If both processed all information in the same manner, then our potential would be severely limited. The two halves of the brain are like two basically similar computers. If they were programmed the same, then each given a learning potential of one, their collective potential would be one plus one or two. But since each half of the brain is programmed differentially and provided with a network of interconnective tissue, one plus one becomes equal to a sum much greater than the parts. This was supported by Dimon in 1971. He demonstrated that, when words were flashed simultaneously to the right and left hemispheres as opposed to each separately, a greater output was exercised.[1] Similar results were obtained by Dimond and Beaumont when visual input was distributed across the hemispheres.[2] They also found that in a perceptual matching task of figures and forms use of both hemispheres produced superior output over the use of either hemisphere alone. Further, when only one hemisphere was used the right produced higher performance than the left.[3] This would indicate that in the interaction and specialization of the two sides of the brain, one plus one equals a sum of infinite quantity which is perhaps one of the greatest secrets of the wonderful organization of the human nervous system.

Recent research indicates that the two halves of the brain do communicate and share information, but we normally "think" or perceive our world from the standpoint of socialized consciousness of left hemisphere dominance. While we consider this sort of thought as consciousness, the right half of the brain also remains active and perfectly capable of responding to the world. It is possible, therefore, as we have seen with the illustration of a walk in the park, to switch the mode of consciousness from left to right. We may also experience a mode of consciousness somewhere in between, as in the case of listening to a story in verbal language and producing pictures through right hemisphere activity. Thus, we shift consciousness from left to right and to many points in between. This ability is much like the functioning of a stereosystem which can be adjusted to the left speaker, the right speaker, or to a point in between with both speakers bringing out different but complimentary sounds.

Modulation of Consciousness

I am handsome, strong, pretty, intelligent, athletic, dumb, or a host of other characteristics. These are left hemispheric evaluations which are primarily socially learned. They are verbal labels which carry some sort of socially learned importance to my self-concept. I see a bird and wonder at his flight, I feel happy in the sunshine, I love to run, I hear a beautiful song, see an exciting picture, and build an unusual and unique art object which I have never seen. Now I am conscious in the right hemisphere. If consciousness returns to the left hemisphere, I will evaluate this nonverbal experience or behavior as being worthwhile, as right or wrong, as important or unimportant.

I am listening to my teacher read a story about Tom Sawyer, and as she talks I turn the words into images of Tom running along the river. I am modulating my consciousness between the left and right hemisphere in order to fully comprehend what I am hearing. Later, I listen only to the words the teacher is saying about how Tom made his mother very unhappy and I focus my attention on left hemispheric self-awareness. But slowly I begin to daydream about an experience I had along a river and the teacher's words become distant until I do not hear them at all. Engaged in a personal and creative fantasy of my own, I have shifted my consciousness to the right hemisphere. Thus we go through each day, sometimes concentrating with left hemispheric consciousness and at other times with right, but always modulating ourselves to some point in between.

The Shadow of Humanness

Apparently, the two hemispheres of the brain can function and perceive without the awareness of the other. Split personality is not unique to psychotic individuals, for there may be duality of being in each of us. Are we not one but two? Individuals who have lost major portions of either hemisphere due to brain injury are able to continue to live and to engage in normal behavior except that certain competencies may cease. Often the opposite hemisphere can even assume some of the functions lost in the damaged hemisphere. Of course this depends on the nature of the function lost, how old the individual is, and a host of other factors too complex to discuss here. Let us review some of the probable functions which appear lateralized into each hemisphere. Many of these are now being researched and much has to be learned, but for our purpose here let it be assumed that these functions are more or less lateralized into these respective hemispheres.

A number of studies indicate that the left hemisphere predominates in functions associated with speech and language (Levy and Trevarthen).[4] Work by Sperry, Gaxxaniga, and Bogen are typical of the interest and recognition of the left hemispheric dominance in language function. This is a viewpoint now widely held by psychoneurologists and neurologists as a consequence of recognizing that in most humans three significant areas of brain structure in the left hemisphere are larger than corresponding areas in the right. These areas include the temporal plate, the portion of Wernicke's area on the convexity, and the cortex in the parietal operculum. The fact that these areas are larger on the left and that they deal with speech and language suggests an anatomical and physiological basis for the predisposition of language in the left hemisphere and subsequent tendency toward left hemisphere dominance in cognition.[5]

One of the most striking differences between the hemispheres is that proposed by Levy-Agresti and Sperry, that the hemispheres proceed by different modes, the left by sequential analytic procedures and the right with synthetic gestalt apperception.[6] Bogen and Bogen attribute special capacities for tonal, timbre, and other aspects of music to the right hemisphere.[7] Bogen and Bogen also suggest explicitly that there are two different modes of thought, propositional and appositional which tend to dominate the activities of the left and right hemispheres respectively.

In 1973 Dimond and Beaumont found a greater variability and ingenuity in the right hemisphere which led them to see that hemisphere as being concerned with the more inventive, exploratory, and improvisatory aspects of mental activity.[8]

Many studies which concern specific aspects of hemispheric function are reported in, *Hemisphere Function in the Human Brain.*[9]

In a more popularized version the functions of the two hemispheres were outlined by Paul Bakan[10] concerning differential hemisphere function. His summated list constructed from a range of research is as follows:

Left Hemisphere	*Right Hemisphere*
Verbal	Preverbal
Analytic	Synthetic
Abstract	Concrete
Rational	Emotional
Temporal	Spatial
Digital	Analogic
Objective	Subjective
Active	Passive
Tense	Relaxed
Euphoric	Depressed
Sympathetic	Parasympathetic
Propositional	Appositional

Bakan's summated list is typical of the tendency of many

writers to attempt to place specific functions within the two hemispheres much as if only such functions occurred in either hemisphere. We accept this general notion but add that our goal in understanding children is to recognize that it is not the qualities of either hemisphere which are significant but the capacity of the brain to integrate and use such capacities through a synthesis of behavior.

In our work we have found that learning and behavioral disorders of children, just as in much of the research dealing with behavior of brain-damaged patients by neurologists, does tend to support the sorts of lateralized functions outlined above. However, for the classroom teacher it may be appropriate to list the sorts of lateralized functions which we find of importance in the classroom. Our own assumptions are outlined here with the recognition that most are supported by research as cited previously while some are inferred from available research. It is a model for basic understanding of the learning behavior of children relative to hemispheric function. Such a model will be important in our later discussions. Further, the descriptions here are those which are usually the case but, as will be discussed later, lateralization does not always occur in the "usual" way.

THE LEFT HEMISPHERE

1. Control of speech and gestures related to speech.
2. Reception, storage, language memory, synthesis of verbal information, language structure and syntax, and verbal meaning.

As a consequence of language function the following factors also relate to left hemisphere control and direction.

3. Awareness and organization of time and serialization of perception and information.
4. Consciousness of time and passing of time in logical sequence, and subsequently, objective thought, order, and logic.
5. Social values and comprehension of values deemed appro-

priate in the culture, social aggression, competition, religious beliefs and attitudes.
6. Understanding and socialization into typical or normal behaviors of the culture.
7. Concept of social or political authority, assertion toward social ascendance, and philosophical thought.
8. Higher math and complex mathematical concept formation.

THE RIGHT HEMISPHERE

1. Recognition and understanding (comprehension) of non-verbal sounds with minor ability in language.
2. Integration of complex motoric coordination and sensitivity to sensory information relating to movement.
3. Recognition of shapes, form-space relationships, behaviors of objects and people, and meaning in nonverbal spatial information.
4. Intuition and insight.
5. Perceptual gestalt and holistic perception and awareness.
6. Inventive, creative, and improvisatory abilities.
7. Recognition and synthesis of musical perception and rhythmic activity.
8. Artistic abilities and appreciation.
9. Simple calculation.

The two hemispheres most likely utilize and put together information into meaningful wholes so that the individual can totally perceive and understand his environment. In essence, the major function of this specialization is the final integration of information from both hemispheres into one meaningful whole. For example, in reading and writing the individual must integrate information from both hemispheres not only to recognize and understand the activity but also to continue to produce verbal and motoric expression. This specialization and eventual integration is perhaps the key to higher human capacities.

But there is a ghost in the machine, a shadow of humanness, that escapes our usual awareness. While both hemispheres function singularly and eventually in union, it is significant to realize that both can function separately. Are there two minds in the being of each of us? Is there an integrated being who finds his awareness dependent upon the function of two separate beings? If we tend to organize our world into language-based rational thoughts, then the left hemisphere is our predominant base of being. We may integrate information from the right hemisphere, but that information is utilized relative to the dictates of the left hemisphere. But the right hemisphere, the natural being of us, continues to "think," to learn, and to grow even though it is forced to submit itself to the whims and needs of the left hemisphere. Is it the natural child in us, the quiet right hemisphere, which is the ghost in the machine? This part of us is always there, always alert, and in ways little known to most of us. What are the implications of this information in relationship to teaching children more effectively, nurturing healthier and happier personalities, and the continuing struggle within ourselves toward personal growth?

There is much to be learned, and further research is necessary before we can be certain of the implications of such research to the teaching of children and the nature of real responsibility which we hold as parents. More significantly, we must learn how such theory limits our own potential as human beings or provides the key to expanded human awareness and actualization. In our discussions we will make rather giant and unsophisticated leaps concerning such implications, without apology, for we have seen significant results with children who have learning disabilities, with socially maladjusted children and adults, and with growing and healthy individuals when we evaluated their behavior and learning, utilizing even the basic information of the theory at present.

We must close this chapter then with a major question. Is each hemisphere capable of separate states of consciousness as has been suggested here? Is it possible that neither the left or right hemisphere is conscious, but that another entity within the brain system provides the basis for the nature of consciousness? Is "consciousness" a thing or a process of neurological activity? If we accept the possibility that consciousness is simply the result of neurological awareness and perception within the cerebral hemispheres, then we must also accept the concept that each of us has two distinct modes of consciousness, one existing in right hemispheric activity and one existing in left hemispheric activity. If this is so, there is a competitive possibility between our two "selves" and duality in all of us. Yet, if consciousness is an entity, a central core of personal perception and volition, then it cannot exist in either hemisphere, but rather must reside in some other area of the brain or, alas, not "in" the brain at all. Is this the ghost in the machine?

For the purposes of this book the question of consciousness, as a consequence of hemispheric activity or as a separate entity from either hemisphere, must be resolved in order to develop some construct of working with children in the processes of learning. In the coming chapters a discussion of the issue will be explored in some depth. If there is a ghost in the machine, then it must be identified. If there is not, then the duality of us all must be accepted.

REFERENCES

1. S. J. Dimond: Hemisphere function and word registration. *J Exp Psychol, 87*:183-186, 1971.
2. S. J. Dimond and J. G. Beaumont: The use of two hemispheres to increase brain capacity. *Nature, 232*:270-271, 1971.
3. S. J. Dimond and J. G. Beaumont: Processing in perceptual integration between and within the cerebral hemispheres. *Br J Psychol, 63*:509-514, 1972.
4. J. Levy and C. Trevarthen: Perceptual, semantic, and phonetic aspects of elementary language processes in split-brain patients. *Brain, 100*:105-118, 1977.
5. Geschwind, N. and Levitsky, W.: Human brain: Left-right asymmetries in temporal speech region. *Science, 161*:186-187, 1968.
6. J. Levy-Agresti and R. W. Sperry: Differential perceptual capacities in major and minor hemispheres. *Proc Natl Acad Sci USA, 61*:1151, 1968.
7. J. E. Bogen and G. M. Bogen: The other side of the brain, III. The corpus callosum and creativity. *Bull Los Angeles Neurol Soc, 34*:191-220, 1969.
8. S. J. Dimond and J. G. Beaumont: Different personality patterns of human cerebral hemispheres. In preparation, 1973.
9. S. J. Dimond and J. G. Beaumont: *Hemisphere Function in the Human Brain.* New York, Halsted Pr, 1974.
10. P. Bakan: The eyes have it. *Psychology Today, 4(11)*:64-97, April, 1971.

Chapter 2

NEUROLOGY AND CONSCIOUSNESS

PSYCHOLOGISTS and educators have found themselves somewhat confounded in recent years by the proliferation of theories about how children learn and how they feel. These theories, ranging from transactional analysis to assertive training in psychology to open education and individualized reading in education, have not provided the "cure-all" that many professionals had hoped for. Both education and psychology have bred new generation specialists who have promised expanded horizons in knowledge of the human psyche and mind. The concepts surrounding right and left mindedness appear to be growing into similar "cults" of dedicated professionals who are embarked on yet another crusade into pseudointellectualism and social change. But, when one reviews the substantial basis for such optimism, there does not appear to be a clear understanding or practical methodology developing which will bring the "brain bilateralization" theory into the clinic or classroom to the benefit of children. There is a ghost in the machine.

There has been a wealth of printed material available concerning cerebral dominance. Robert Ornstein (of the Langley-Porter Neuropsychiatric Institute at the California Medical Center) is one of the most prominent proponents and researchers of the "new psychology" surrounding the right-mindedness movement. In his book, *The Pyschology of Consciousness*, Doctor Ornstein proposed, based on electroencephalographic research, that the two hemispheres, aside from lateralizing many neurological functions, also appear to exhibit duality in consciousness.[1] In a recent article in *Education Today*, Madeline Hunter (a principal at the University School of the University of California) discussed the practical problems of having right-brained children in left-brained schools.[2] In the June 1976 issue of *Human Behavior*, Wayne

19

Sage reviewed much of the research on differentiated brain function and its relation to learning and behavior.[3] One of the most noted researchers, Roger W. Sperry (of the California Institute of Technology) has spent many years attempting to explore the psyche not in his subjects' verbal ramblings but in the physiology of their brains. He feels he has found two distinctly different consciousnesses that are more than the neurological circuits through which they channel. Says Doctor Sperry "The term *mental forces* would seem appropriate." Doctor Wilder Penfield, noted neurosurgeon, has spent much of his life attempting to demonstrate that the major basis for concepts of "mind" or consciousness lies primarily in the physical functions of the brain and that the mind and the brain are the same entity, but he concludes in his most recent book, *Mystery of the Mind:*

> By listening to patients as they describe an experiential flashback, one can understand the complexity and efficiency of the reflex coordinating and integrative action of the brain. In it, the automatic computer and the highest brain-mechanism play interactive roles, selectively inhibitory and purposeful.

> Does this explain the action of the mind? Can reflex action, in the end, account for it? After years of studying the emerging mechanisms within the human brain, my own answer is "no." Mind comes into action and goes out of action with the highest brain-mechanism, it is true. But the mind has energy. The form of that energy is different from that of neuronal potentials that travel the axone pathways. There I must leave it.[4]

Doctor Penfield, like Doctor Sperry, comes to the conclusion (after years of research to prove the contrary) that so called "mind" or consciousness appears somehow separate and distinct from the neurological activity within the brain itself. There is a ghost in the machine. This has important implications for the concept of "right-mindedness" and "left-mindedness." In the preceding chapter many of the most popular theories about brain bilateralization and specific function were summated in two lists. The general direction of much of the literature on this subject is to imply the existence of not only differentiated neurological function in the two hemispheres but separate consciousnesses as well. While this construct can have important implications in education, our experience with children in the clinic and school settings suggests that there is more to the construct than mere bilateralization of consciousness. In the following discussion we will add our theories to the boiling controversy with the belief that they will serve to assist our own presentation and be, at least, as respectably reliable as others advocated by professionals cited here.

In Figure 1, a simple overview of the central nervous system is illustrated. Our concern is with the three major sections of the system: the spinal cord and lower brain centers; the brain stem; and the cortical hemispheres. The spinal cord and lower brain stem are required for much of the reflective and automatic function within the central nervous system. Reflex behavior and control of involuntary functions such as heart rate, respiration, and balance occur in these centers. The central nervous system is composed of different types of nerve tissue or neurons which function on an electrochemical firing basis receiving information and sending orders to and from the various parts of the body. The young infant, as we will discuss in more detail later, is equipped with many reflex and involuntary behaviors at birth. All else has to be learned through the functions of the brain stem and cortical hemispheres as he gains experience during his first few years.

The brain stem, while involved in many complex functions, has three major activities which are of interest here. Doctor Penfield describes[4] two major functions of specialized centers in the brain stem which are significant to consciousness and general behavioral activity. The first center, the automatic sensory-motor mechanism is a computer integration center for sensory motor information coming to and from the cerebral cortex. The second center, the highest brain mechanism appears to be an integrative center for information going to and from certain areas of the two hemispheres.

It is important to realize that contrary to what many believe, the cerebral hemispheres are not separate entities which are on

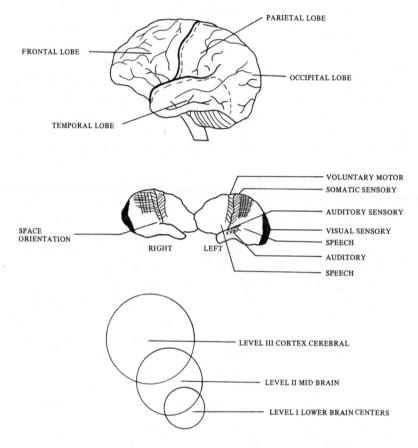

Figure 1: Various areas of functioning in central nervous system.

top of the brain stem but rather elaborations much like a bal-
looning out of the brain stem itself. Further, it is generally
believed that the connection between the two hemispheres, the
corpus callosum, is the major route of interhemispheric communication. In split brain operations it is this connection
which is cut and which often appears to give separate but intact
consciousness in the right and left hemispheres. Many theories
of cerebral integration which attribute the ability of the
two hemispheres to share information are built on the construct that this is possible through the interhemispheric connection, the corpus callosum. We will return to this point

shortly.

The cerebral hemispheres have been "mapped" for specific areas of function by many individuals including Doctor Penfield and Doctor D. O. Hebb.[5] It is well known that the rear of the two hemispheres is the center for visual reception and integration, with a section toward the middle responsible for sensory motor integration, and the frontal portion dealing with a wide range of functions including foresight, some visual activity, and memory. At the side of the left hemisphere are located many areas dealing with auditory processing and speech, while the outer side of the right hemisphere appears to deal mostly with visual and spatial information. This mapping of specific function provided some of the earliest suggestion of the bilateralization of function in the two hemispheres.

Many of the areas of the cerebral hemispheres appear committed at birth to the various functions described here. Yet, according to Penfield, there are important exceptions to the concept of specialized and committed function in certain areas of the hemispheres, as his research located areas in both temporal regions of each hemisphere and in the prefrontal lobes which were apparently not committed to function at birth. The degree of this uncommitted cortical tissue greatly exceeds that of any other animal.

Doctor Penfield labels the uncommitted tissue in the right and left temporal lobes as the "interpretive cortex" and suggests that this center deals with a "stream of consciousness" relating past experience with present. It is here that imagery from past experience is excited and brought to consciousness. Thus, these two areas provide that important ability to recall past experience and relate it to presently occurring experience allowing the complex decisions of which only man appears capable. Further, Doctor Penfield discovered that an area in the prefrontal lobes appears to be related to planned initiative, i.e. the capacity to direct and predict one's behavior in ego-centered ways.

The functions of the highest brain mechanism and the sensory-motor mechanisms are performed as a pre-wired system. Sensory information coming from the various regions of the body are channeled into the automatic sensory-motor mechanism and from there to the cortex regions which receive sensory information and relay back motor commands. Recognition and interpretation of such information is accomplished through this mechanism. Yet, the automatic sensory-motor mechanism seems to function much like a computer. It needs to be programmed. Programming of this computer is accomplished via the directions of the highest brain mechanism. The highest brain mechanism is the integrating point for information coming from the interpretative cortex in each hemisphere; the highest brain mechanism is that point of neurological connection between the sensory motor system of the body and the cortical regions of the two hemispheres now called the interpretative and prefrontal cortex areas. Doctor Penfield has discovered that there are no direct neurological connections between the areas served by the automatic sensory-motor mechanism cortex areas and the interpretative and prefrontal areas. This has significant implications, for it means that those areas must gain awareness of sensory information through the highest brain mechanism in the brain stem. Further, directions and decisions concerning response are channeled from the interpretative cortex through the highest brain mechanism to the automatic sensory-motor mechanism. This suggests that consciousness and planned initiative are actualized by forwarding directions to the highest brain mechanism, which in turn "programs" or directs the automatic sensory-motor mechanism computer to perform specific acts or initiate certain responses. The automatic sensory-motor mechanism computer is the information channel for what is occurring within and about the body, but the highest brain mechanism is the center through which incoming information and outgoing decisions made by the consciousness activity areas are channeled. For the moment, if we consider that the interpretative cortex in each hemisphere, the prefrontal lobes, and some other minor cortical areas appear to be the centers of consciousness, then what we commonly refer to as "self" is neurologically separate from the mechanisms which operate the body. The body is like a container, a physical structure which is controlled by the self.

Consciousness then appears to exist in the neurological function of the right and left hemisphere cortex regions encompassing the interpretative cortex, the prefrontal lobes, and other associated areas not committed to automatic perceptual and sensory processing. Is the collective function of these nonsensory areas the place of mind, of consciousness, and of awareness? Are these areas the ghost in the machine that directs it and gives our being meaning? No, as Doctor Penfield stated, these areas do not seem to provide a basis for the existence of consciousness or of mind. In neither the left nor the right cortex are there areas of neurological function which can account for the nature of mind or consciousness. This is of utmost importance in our emerging concepts of right mindedness and left mindedness, for some researchers suggest that there is a consciousness in both the left and right hemisphere, that there is, in effect, two beings within the body of each of us. This is the foundation upon which much of the notion of right and left mindedness rests. The research of Doctor Penfield and others suggests that one cannot define the functions of either the right or left hemisphere as being the seat of consciousness.

A construct of consciousness, the highest brain mechanism and the automatic sensory-motor mechanism are illustrated in Figure 2. It has been demonstrated that the highest brain mechanism acts as a sort of executive for the interpretative areas of the cortex. Decisions made within consciousness appear to be channeled through the automatic sensory-motor mechanism and the highest brain mechanism. But the highest brain mechanism also acts as a screening system and an alerting system for the consciousness areas. For example, when the highest brain mechanism cuts off sensory information to the consciousness areas we go to sleep and for all practical purposes the "mind" becomes nonfunctional. In the morning, it is the highest brain mechanism executive which activates or awakens the consciousness system. There are other areas of the brain involved in this process but our purpose here is not to argue specific brain function but to merely provide a general overview of function for the teacher or professional involved in teaching children.

It was Penfield's assumption that if consciousness existed as

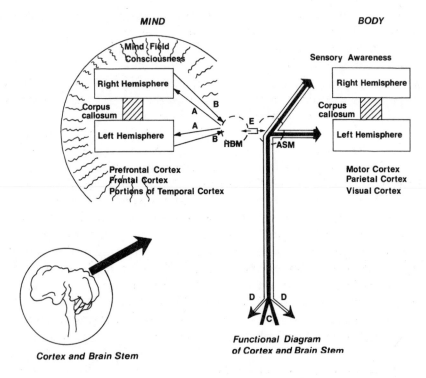

Figure 2: Model of separation of the highest brain mechanism (HBM) and automatic sensory motor mechanism (ASM). Sensory information enters the system (C) and is channeled to the cortex areas involving the motor, parietal, and visual cortex along with some portions of the temporal lobes. The ASM in the brain stem channels this information to the sensory areas and motor responses result (D). Such information is available to the HBM and is channeled to areas in the frontal and temporal lobes where it is perceived as conscious information. The two frontal portions of the right and left hemispheres provide the energy for the phenomenon of consciousness, which then forwards directions to the HBM. This center is in direct contact with the ASM which then acts upon the information (E). This point of interaction provides the link of communications between consciousness and the sensory motor systems. Thought can be generally activated in the "conscious areas" of the brain without involvement of the sensory motor system, just as the sensory motor system can function without the conscious awareness of the frontal areas. This makes for a separation of "Mind" and "Body" which has often been of concern in learning processes. (A) and (B) display the incoming and outgoing communications between the HBM and the conscious portions of the cortex.

a function of the interpretative cortex and associated areas, then when one electrically stimulated those portions of the brain the individual would respond by feeling alert and aware of whatever memory traces and experiences were being tapped. In essence, consciousness would be artificially stimulated by the electrode just as the highest brain mechanism appears to be. But from this sort of experimentation and other research Penfield had to conclude quite different probabilities. A stream of consciousness was activated in patients who were still awake during the operative research. But, unexpectedly, they were able to interpret their artificially stimulated stream of consciousness as if *they* were viewing it. The electrode did activate a flow of conscious experience, but if these areas of the brain were the same as the so called "mind" how could the patient also appear to be conscious to the present situation when the neurons were being used for the past experience? Penfield states, "He is aware of what is going on in the operating room as well as the 'flashback' from the past. The stream of consciousness is suddenly doubled for him." Penfield summarizes:

> The patient's mind, which is considering the situation in such an aloof and critical manner, can only be something apart from neuronal reflex action. It is noteworthy that two streams of consciousness are flowing, the one driven by input from the environment, the other by an electrode delivering sixty impulses per second to the cortex. The fact that there should be no confusion in the consciousness state suggests that, although the content of consciousness depends in large measure on neuronal activity, awareness does not.

> One may ask this question: does the highest brain mechanism provide the mind with its energy, an energy in such changed form that it no longer needs to be conducted along neuro-axones? To ask such a question is, I fear, to run the risk of hollow laughter from the physicists.[4]

The real issue for Penfield and others has been that age-old question of the separation of mind and body. In the foregoing discussion Doctor Penfield, like Doctor Sperry, is forced to suggest that the so-called mind or consciousness appears to exist separately from the brain system. What affect does this have on the right-minded and left-minded construct? If the "mind" or consciousness does not arise from the interpretative or other surrounding tissues in the temporal and frontal lobes, then the self or consciousness must arise from some other source. Further, if consciousness cannot be "fixed" in the right hemisphere, then surgical separation of it by way of surgical elimination of the corpus collosum is less than probable.

Before we proceed further, let us take a moment to review and summarize what has been said thus far:

A. There are three major units within the central nervous system: the spinal cord and lower brain stem, the brain stem, and the cerebral hemispheres.

B. The lower brain stem provides much of the reflexive action in early life and provides much of the control of involuntary activity in the body. It is the body's most immediate supervisor.

C. The brain stem includes the automatic sensory-motor "computer" and the highest brain mechanism. Sensory information coming from within the body and from the environment (aside from some diversions in the lower brain stem and associated structures such as the medulla) is channeled into the automatic sensory-motor mechanism and then on to the regions in the cerebral cortex committed to process such information. The highest brain mechanism is the executive and transmission center for information from the automatic sensory-motor mechanism to the interpretative and consciousness oriented centers of the cortex. It is through the highest brain mechanism that information is received in consciousness and through which the consciousness programs or directs the computor. The highest brain mechanism can inhibit information from going to the conscious areas of the cortex, but it serves primarily as an executive of the consciousness.

D. The sensory motor functions of the body are learned through repetition and practice to become much like a bank of specific and complex programs which can be activated by the conscious (temporal interpretive cortex, prefrontal cortex and other associated areas) via the conscious executive, the highest brain mechanism.

E. The automatic sensory motor mechanism can carry out short-term directions from the highest brain mechanism, but without constant mediation and direction from the highest brain mechanism, specific decisions cannot be made by the automatic sensory-motor mechanism. This process may be called mediation of behavior.

F. The concept of "mind" has been thought to be a function of cortical activity in the interpretive and prefrontal areas. But research by Penfield and Sperry suggests that the "mind" or conscious stream of awareness appears to have an energy base separate from these areas of the cortex.

The teacher in tomorrow's schools will need a much broader conceptual basis if he is to understand and apply these theories. One final note should be made about the concept of "mind." Since the conclusions of Penfield and Sperry appear to be a metaphysical entity rather than a neurological one, it may be safe to presume that there is a "mind" and "body" and that the intent of effective education is to teach and serve the needs of both. A metaphysical concept of mind may not serve to give us as much concreteness as is needed in work with children, but the metaphysical notion of mind may have significant implications for understanding much of the current theory about left and right mindedness which, at this point, apparently is presumed by many researchers to be a concept of duality in consciousness.

One of the central questions in the first chapter was the existence or nonexistence of a duality of being in each of us. There seemed to be something missing in that notion. We choose to call that something the shadow of humanness, the ghost in the machine. We submit that there is, through the function of the central nervous system, a higher state of awareness created that may be called a "bioenergy field" or, in the theory of Robert Ornstein, "a Mind Field."[6] We choose to call this phenomenon the "bioenergy field." While oversimplified, it is much like light given off when electrical energy is transformed into thermal energy in the light bulb. Beyond the electrical and thermal energy, which science can explain easily, there is the problem of light which is less easily explained though it can be measured and observed. While the theories of electrical and thermal energy and the transformation of energy can be explained, magnetism is less accessible through present knowledge. It is our presumption here that the so-called "mind" or bioenergy field existing within the brain is a product of neuronic energy but that, as with the case of light or magnetic energy, it exists beyond the basis for its creation and that this energy once activated, through the functions of the central nervous system, is capable of control of its own creative source.

The bioenergy field, illustrated in Figure 2, becomes then the essence of selfness and awareness. But it is dependent for both its energy and capacity upon the effectiveness and competency of the central nervous system. How the central nervous system functions relative to integrative capabilities will, in no small measure, determine both the nature and quality of the bioenergy field or the self-consciousness. Certainly, it can be guessed that the nature of personality then is closely tied to the nature of the bioenergy field. Since this field is dependent upon the integrities of the central nervous system, insults from the environment such as drugs, nutritional deficiencies, disease, and brain dysfunction or injury can alter drastically the nature and quality of the bioenergy field. There is much to be learned and we admit that the oversimplification of central nervous system function here is less than acceptable for psychoneurological clarification. Our purpose is to give an overview for the teacher and not to debate the great issues yet to be resolved in psychoneurology. We will leave that to professionals in neurology and psychology. We want to build a model behavior which can be applied in practical situations in the classroom until more detailed research can be accumulated by those following Penfield. He has but opened the door for us.

The Issue of Right and Left Mindedness

The ghost in the machine, then, is the bioenergy field which supercedes in no small degree the limited concept that there are two consciousnesses, one in the right hemisphere and one in the left hemisphere. Consciousness, according to our own viewpoint, exists not in the hemispheres but somewhere throughout the hemispheres as a separate but unitary entity, and it is dependent upon the information and function of the two hemispheres. Thus, higher capacities, i.e. stronger influence, in one hemisphere or the other may then provide more influence on the bioenergy field than the opposing and less competent hemisphere. This has the effect of giving the bioenergy field a distinct orientation favoring that flow of information which is the most predominant, i.e. left mindedness or right mindedness. The central issue is that there is not a dichotomy of consciousness as many of the current researchers favor; rather, there is but one awareness, one consciousness, which modulates between right or left hemispheric informational banks, now right minded, now left minded, and predominantly oriented toward that bank which provides the most energy and informational access. For example, in split brain research, one never reads of an individual who remained only in the right or left mode but rather individuals who did not seem to know what was going on in the opposing hemisphere while being oriented to the other hemisphere. In split brain research there have been no instances of simultaneous awareness in both halves of the brain. It is not, therefore, the hemispheres which contain separate consciousness, but rather the real consciousness, the bioenergy field, is activated first by one hemisphere and then the other. If the corpus callosum is intact, then a flow of information can occur between the two hemispheres and the bioenergy field can utilize this integrated information simultaneously. But when the connective communication tissue is cut, apparently the bioenergy field moves from one hemisphere to the other, never being able to simultaneously integrate the information. The split brain then affects the efficiency of the bioenergy field but not the bioenergy field itself.

For the purposes of this book, then, consciousness is perceived as a separate entity from hemispheric activity though it is dependent upon that for the quality of conscious capabilities. A semantic problem exists when the terms *consciousness, awareness, thought* or *thinking*, and *perception* are used and a distinction between these terms is necessary for our purposes.

Consciousness is used to mean an awareness by the individual of his own thoughts and the exercising of some form of decision activity or contemplation of specific information. The act of contemplation may be defined as the exercise of volition upon the environment or self. *Awareness* exists in this activity, but awareness also exists within hemispheric activity aside from consciousness. For example, I may be "lost" in contemplation of a personal problem while at the same time some area of the central nervous system, i.e. the hemispheres, the sensory motor system, or the reflexive system, may also be perceptually aware of environmental or internal body information. The specific center of the central nervous system which is aware of particular environmental information may respond to that information without my conscious control or response. Thus, in the case of consciousness, awareness is the personal perception of voluntary behavior, while in the case of the nonconscious center, awareness is more a matter of reflexive or learned conditioned response. Awareness implies a state of receptivity and perception, but the locus of control of that awareness may be within consciousness or it may be in a nonconscious central nervous system entity. In this sense, awareness may occur simultaneously in consciousness and in a nonconscious entity, but only in the former is awareness tied to the act of personal volition.

Thinking then becomes a characteristic of consciousness and not a nonconscious activity existing within the central nervous system. From this it would be our conclusion that when thinking occurs it is the bioenergy field which "thinks" and not the central nervous system or one of its parts. Cognition, then, is a process of consciousness and not merely a psychoneurological process arising from the activity of the central nervous system itself.

There are many implications to be gained by the teacher in the preceding discussion of neurological theory. Obviously, the argument concerning the nature of consciousness and the function of the brain will continue, and the outcomes of such research and discussion will not be felt in education for some time to come. Yet, there is an increasing interest and involvement in the practical aspects of the left and right minded theory currently being presented in popular and educational literature. Some of the implications concerning this interest need to be outlined here. The most that we can do as educators and psychologists is to speculate how, in the classroom and clinic, the available research can be used rationally with children both in normal development and in cases of learning or personality difficulties. If the theory has some practical applications which can demonstrate, in some manner, an effective aid or method in teaching children, then we should apply the theory.

The Mind-Body Phenomenon

In later sections of the book we will spend some time presenting concepts of perceptual motor development and their importance to learning in the classroom. It would appear that there is at least a general neurological principle operating in learning which relates to the theory of the highest brain mechanism and the automatic sensory motor mechanism. Learned patterns of motor behavior and integrated sensory motor information must be "programmed" through the perception of the highest brain mechanism and/or consciousness.

The young infant must learn to move, to walk, and to perform many complex motoric activities which are specific to his cultural and learning environment. For example, learning to make forms, letters, and general movements during various learning activities must all be done while the child is "consciously" attending to language and environmentally based concerns or instructions rather than to the motoric operations themselves. Specific examples of attending to language rather than to motoric operations include the process of taking a spelling test or writing a term paper. The child has to perform writing movements while attending mentally to the sequence of the words or thoughts. The child's conscious stream of thought must be focused upon content rather than form, and he must concentrate on the thought behind the writing instead of on the writing skill itself. In this activity the automatic sensory-motor mechanism is carrying out prelearned motoric programs and patterns without the conscious attention of the highest brain mechanism. The highest brain mechanism is busy processing information and synthesizing thoughts coming from the hemi-spheres and relaying directions, i.e. programs, to the automatic sensory-motor mechanisms which are then carried out by the sensory motor system while the highest brain mechanism con-tinues to process the coming directions.

When a child has not learned, through repetition and prac-tice, the many motor patterns needed to write in an automatic way, he has to stop after each thought and divert his attention to the direction of the sensory-motor system. This interruption in his thought pattern not only often tends to destroy the thought but also prevents the child from working fast enough to keep up with the spelling exam. We have observed many other difficulties in this disruption of the thought pattern. When the child shifts his attention from directing the sensory-motor system in making a letter back to the thought pattern he often misses some of his original pattern and leaves out letters, reverses the order of letters, or misspells words without his "conscious" awareness that he has done so. The minimal diffi-culty that can result from this lack of integration is writing so poorly produced that it is illegible in any case. Many of these children are often seen as children with spelling problems, language disorders, or even poor intelligence when in fact they have a lack of learned proficiency in the automatic sensory-motor system. This lack will be discussed in some detail in later sections dealing with classroom learning difficulties.

A classic problem we have observed and one which often prompts teachers and parents to feel a child is "hyperactive" is also related to the lack of integration and efficiency in function between the highest brain mechanism and the automatic sensory-motor mechanism. If the child has not learned effective patterns of motor control which can be set into motion through directives of the highest brain mechanism, when the child di-verts his attention away from the motor system, the system goes into what we call "random meandering." This is the child who appears restless, who moves about constantly during reading or conversation, or who has great difficulty keeping himself "still" at times. For example, the child is asked a question while he is engaged in some motor act such as copying, drawing a picture, or making something with his hands. He does not answer the question and does not seem to hear. But, if we watch him at this moment, he is not only preoccupied with the activity, he is not as restless and active as we often see him. When we finally get his attention he not only listens to us or talks to us but begins the characteristic movements of shifting in his seat, moving his hands, and touching things. This random movement is a result of poor integration of the two systems, consciousness and motoric control. If he is engaged in a motoric act his highest brain mechanism and consciousness is directing the motor function through a step-by-step series of neurological messages. But when we ask him to focus on language or verbal content he has to shift his attention to that mode and thereby leaves the sensory-motor system without the constant monitoring it was receiving during the motor activity. Without the continued direction the motor system moves almost at random or without specific direction. In most children a message, "relax all systems," can be sent and the motor system will relax and remain on standby until it receives further directions. Through many years of practice and "building up" sensory-motor programming, the child's motoric activities can be directed. But, if the child is poorly coordinated, i.e. has not developed specific programs, then the motor system begins to simply wander about much like a car without a driver. Again, this problem will be discussed later along with other implications of the left and right minded theory.

Developmental Mind-Body Relationships

The foregoing discussion suggests, for purposes of educational programming, that the teacher conceptualize the child's growth and functioning within the "mind-body" duality viewpoint. This is to say that the child has special needs in perceptual-motor development which relate to learning specific motoric patterns. The sensory-motor patterns related to formal learning must be developed to the automatic level so that the child can focus his attention upon the content of learning as opposed to the mechanical expression of that knowledge. Ineffective sensory or perceptual motor functioning inhibits and even prevents language and formalized learning behaviors. Yet, there is a critical relationship between the development of effective language patterns and formal thought and the sensory-motor basis of learning. While there is a need to understand the operational differences between formalized thought and sensory-motor expression, there is also a need to understand the developmental relationships between sensory-motor development and subsequent language and formalized learning. In the case of developmental concepts, one cannot as easily deal with a mind-body duality since both develop in an integrated and interdependent manner. In the following chapters we will discuss both the operational problems between mind and body functions in learning and the difficulties in development as the two areas proceed toward higher levels of maturation.

Motoric Dominance and Learning

The concepts of hemisphericity and consciousness present a difficult learning task for the classroom teacher, but additional elements of cognitive and perceptual functioning also include the role of motoric dominance in both sensory-motor development and hemisphericity in consciousness. In recent years much attention has been given to problems of motor dominance and performance in learning to read and write. When one considers the implications of hemisphericity on behavior and learning, the effects of motoric dominance and kinesthetic capacities must also play a critical role. There is little doubt that education is oriented toward the left minded and right-handed child. We have not considered this additional factor thus far in our discussion. In the coming chapters we will add this dimension of development to the concept of hemisphericity to broaden the theory of development and learning to the right and left minded problem.

In the remaining chapters we will refer to children with right and left mindedness though, as mentioned here, we recognize that this reference suggests that the child is operating from a predominantly left or right hemispheric orientation rather than from an actual duality of consciousness. At this point such a minor difference between our own theory and that of others advocating the right and left mindedness appears unimportant. As we proceed through our discussion it should become more obvious why such a difference in theory is of importance in discussion of educational and learning problems. Much of the present literature is designed to understand the nature of consciousness alone. Our intent is to broaden this concept into the educational field.

REFERENCES

1. R. E. Ornstein: *The Psychology of Consciousness*. New York, Grossman, 1976.
2. M. Hunter: Right brained kids in left brained schools. *Today's Education*, 65:45-48, Nov-Dec 1976.
3. W. Sage: The split brain lab. *Human Behavior*, June, 1976.
4. W. Penfield: *The Mystery Of The Mind*. Princeton, Princeton U Pr, 5:24, 1975.
5. D. O. Hebb: *Introduction to Psychology*. Philadelphia, Saunders, 1966.
6. R. E. Ornstein: *Mind Field*. New York, Grossman, 1976.

Chapter 3

EARLY DEVELOPMENT OF NATURALIZED
AND SOCIALIZED BEHAVIORS

THE naturalness of early childhood is evident in the tendency of young children to state their impressions as they perceive them without social values or logical critical analysis interfering. This is one of the characteristics of childhood that both amuses us as adults and often catches us by surprise when the child states frankly what should be obvious. In the story of "The Emperor's New Clothes" it was a child who finally stated that the emperor was wearing little more than his birthday suit. The child had not learned social conformity, nor did he understand the subtle implications of stating the reality of what he saw. During the first few years of life, children are first occupied with learning to walk, to move about, and to control and understand their basic sensory world. Only as some control is gained over the motoric and sensory world can the child turn his attention to language and the cultural task of learning values. It is right hemispheric consciousness that assumes priority in early childhood experiences. Concrete sensory information of sight, sound, touch, taste, smell, and kinesthetic awareness do not deceive as easily as do words. It may be said, then, that our most natural state of consciousness is early experience in right hemispheric thought and organization. It is the fundamental structure in all of life. Language is a more complex and learned behavior, even though the neurological basis for its development may exist latently during those first months and years.

As the child begins to use language to a greater extent to represent sensory experience, left hemispheric function develops toward eventual dominance in brain function and consciousness. Language, with its logical organization and demand for structuring sensory experience, eventually becomes the predominant expression of thought and consciousness in most individuals. Language carries the values of the culture and gives the clarity for assisting the child in learning how to behave appropriately in groups. One might ask why a child would give up his carefree world of natural behavior for the conditioning of linguistically based values and inhibitors on behavior. There are at least two major reasons: the child's tendency to seek even higher levels of knowledge and, consequently, personal control; and the overriding fact that, as the child grows into his fifth and sixth year, social rewards are based primarily on linguistic skills. The child must learn to behave appropriately to the values of the culture, along with learning the educational skills of writing and reading, if he is to be accepted at home, in school, and on the playground. Social conditioning and rewards finally subordinate the natural consciousness. As we will see in later chapters, accidental interventions in this process of Freudian socialization can cause ramifications not only in the personality of the child but in his ability to learn or adjust.

There is a subtle process here which must be recognized by parents and teachers. Neurologically, the left hemispheric motor cortex contains a region which controls the right side of the body, while the right hemisphere motor cortex gives direction to the left side of the body. Each individual must, during the first few years of life, establish one or the other motor cortex as the dominant side in general movement. This is one of the most significant developmental milestones and is usually accomplished by the age of three and certainly by the age of four years. The child must have this initial period from approximately birth to three or four years in which the basic motor and sensory areas of development can mature prior to extensive language activity. Teachers and parents of young children have long been aware that language development appears to level off or even regress when a child is learning to walk or to engage in the acquisition of some motor skill. This regression does not occur nearly so often after the age of five years since the sensory and motor systems are finally mature enough so that less time must be spent in their control and expression. The most intense learning period of expressive language begins around the end of the third year and proceeds rapidly into the sixth year. By the time the child is seven, he is displaying much general capacity in both sensory and motor areas along with language usage. During this period less and less time is spent in natural consciousness and increasingly more in socialized function. It is during this period of three to seven years of age that many children experience great frustrations due to the problems involved in increased motoric and language sophistication required by both parents and teachers. The child who is developing well will learn to integrate these two modes of function, and development proceeds normally. However, the child who is experiencing delayed control in motor function often has great difficulties with language. Conversely, the child who has, for genetic and/or environmental reasons, developed a sophisticated language system may have done so at the expense of naturalistic functions. We often find a verbally bright child who has extremely poor fine motor control and other sensory-based deficiencies.

A major developmental milestone for the six-year-old child is that both hemispheres reach a consonant level of maturity and capacity, a development necessary in order for the child to function well in social and educational areas. Unfortunately, many children in the first grade may not display equal competencies in both modes of behavior. This can cause social, personality, and educational problems. It is important to understand that both modes of consciousness must develop adequately in order for the individual to assume a posture of successful school and social behavior. If one or the other hemisphere has gross inadequacies due to genetic, environmental, or emotional factors, then this imbalance will surely shape both the child's learning capabilities and his personality into directions which are atypical for most children. Such difficulties cause the teacher and the parent increasing frustration in meeting the child's needs. His behavior and learning patterns may become so deviant from the normal expectations that learning disabilities or emotional disturbance may be suspected. The child is neither deviant nor disturbed; he is different. The culture is totally unprepared to deal with this unusual and often frustrating child.

HEMISPHERIC DEVELOPMENTAL CONCEPTS

Left and Right Mindedness

I am a member of my family and we live in Normaltown where I attend elementary school. I am ten years old, typical for my age in size and general interests. I do well in school, and I often make very good grades which my parents tell me will help when I go to college. I believe in God and attend church every Sunday with my parents and sisters and brothers. My father is an accountant and works very hard to be a good citizen. I am a boy and I play baseball. I have many friends, and the community we live in is a neat and good place to live. I live in America and wish that all of the world could live like we do so all children would be as lucky as I am.

So speaks the consciousness in the socialized mode. Here we see indications of significant left hemispheric consciousness and cultural training. There is evidence of holding social values, of grasping time and sequence, of being able to identify with places which are both specific and general but which all have names that give them meaning. The child shows his verbal ability in describing himself and his place in time and space, and he evidences logic and personal meaning in his language and values of the culture. Perception of past and future events, each based on the ability to perceive, through language, the concept of time and space, is also indicated. This child has been nurtured by the Western culture with its emphasis on the rational and on the use of language to evaluate oneself and the environment. This mode of behavior is referred to as "left mindedness."

I love the feeling of running and simply lying on the grass. I make up stories in which people don't talk but everyone knows what each is thinking. I race to distant places in a moment and live in tomorrow and yesterday as if they were today. I become an eagle and a river, I grow in size and become smaller than a mouse, I imagine building a great tower and create images in my mind which I have never seen before. I seem to sense things before they happen, and I feel a relationship with things that happened before I was born. I reflect quietly on myself and learn about the world without reading or going to school. I have secret places I can hide and funny beings to talk to which no one else knows or sees. I have great determination to do what I will, and I am full of love and hate all at once. I love to be touched and to touch back for it makes me feel good. I watch what people do and know what they think. I make things without reading the directions and often get into trouble because I'm late or forget what time it is. Teachers get upset when I don't finish my work and everyone is concerned about grades which don't seem very important to me.

So speaks consciousness in the naturalistic mode. He demonstrates experiences of timeless space, a lack of organization and responsibility. There is no concern for convention and for the values which everyone holds to be so important, but there is imagination and creativity, problem-solving through development of unconventional alternates never before imagined. A proclivity toward self-indulgence, determination to perform one's will, and an unbounded desire to feel and experience all that surrounds the individual are the characteristics of the naturalistic child. He shows a sensitivity to sound and rhythm, an ability to experience sensory aspects of the environment, and the desire to seek out new experience simply for the feeling of it. This is an Eastern cultural characteristic for it is intuitive, self-reflective and nonverbal, nearly the opposite of Western culture thought for it is void of language and conventional values. This sort of behavior mode is referred to as "right mindedness."

THE CEREBRAL DISSONANCE THEORY

The natural child, a "right minded" unconventional child, is a child who, while he should have gained some level of integrated ability in both modes of thought, develops an unusual mode dominance in which naturalized thought becomes the primary mode of consciousness. If a child utilizes naturalistic thoughts as his primary mode of consciousness instead of the usual socialized mode, he tends to have difficulty with values, time and sequence, behavioral organization, and language. Because of these difficulties, he is frequently the subject of clinical testing and assistance.

Bobby was a nine year old boy who was brought to the clinic by his parents at the request of the teacher because of his disruptive behavior and poor school work. The teacher suspected that he had some sort of learning disability and/or that he was experiencing a severe emotional problem. We have seen many boys like Bobby who, due to poor parenting and home conditions, have not become well socialized and are unable to follow directions, who develop poor peer relationships, or who have difficulty adhering to the rules of the school. In such cases there is often a serious emotional problem which requires the assistance of a mental health professional for both the parents and the boy. But Bobby was one of those boys who displayed what we now call *cerebral dissonance syndrome*.

Bobby was quite receptive to the testing and often laughed and joked with us. He was very observant and appeared to be quite intelligent. He was intelligent, but in a very special way. His general verbal or language abilities placed him in the high normal range of intelligence, but his nonverbal or performance abilities were well into the upper gifted range. For many years psychologists have suspected that wide differences in verbal and performance intelligence scores were either an indication of emotional problems or of organic brain dysfunction. But Bobby displayed neither of these deficits, though inappropriate or hasty conclusions might have been made in this direction. His parents commented that he could build elaborate structures from building blocks and that he seemed highly capable of working with mechanical things. He was the pitcher on his Little League baseball team and had shown excellent coordination even as a very young child. He still persisted in drawing at school when he should be completing his assignments. He spent much of his time daydreaming and often would not pay attention in class. He did not distract other children, but he seemed quite distractable himself. His parents stated that he often forgot the names of places they went on vacation, but he could tell you all sorts of things about where he had been, what he did, and specific information which the parents had long forgotten. He would watch television for hours, and the parents felt that perhaps his fascination for television was one of the reasons he was so disinterested in reading.

In psychological and developmental testing, children are asked questions about words, questions requiring abstract thought, questions requiring mathematical or logical thought, and questions requiring factual information. This yields some idea of the child's verbal capacity. During this sort of testing, Bobby was somewhat distractable and uninterested although he did demonstrate at least average capabilities in verbal skills. During performance testing, Bobby became intensely interested and appeared to want to solve each problem before giving up. These tests involved making designs with blocks, arranging series of a picture into logical stories, working puzzles, and recognizing missing parts in pictures. Further, Bobby scored exceptionally high on tests that required drawing a person, reproducing forms from memory, and in creative problem solving. The significant aspect of this sort of behavior is that Bobby was only average in those functions which primarily involved socialized or language function, but in naturalistic or nonverbal functions he was exceptionally bright and capable.

Bobby is a natural child unchained and an alien in a world of "left minded" people. His predominant mode of consciousness is that of naturalistic function. Bobby is a different sort of human being who has trouble with language not because he is incompetent in socialized capacity but because he is so highly capable in the opposite function, that of the naturalistic thought. When Bobby sees the world, his first response is to pay attention to what he sees from a naturalistic viewpoint because, for him, that is the most meaningful way to understand. He sees the structure in words but misses their phonetic meaning. He daydreams about flying an airplane instead of understanding what a story was actually saying about an airplane. Bobby loves television, for he can understand most of it through watching the movement, the form, and the behavior of people rather than listening to what they say.

Bobby as a young child, developed language late though this is not always the case with children who display this syndrome. Bobby's mode of thought process also had other interesting features in behavioral situations outside the formal testing environment. He had difficulty learning to tell time, remembering the order of the days of the week, in serialization, or in placing things in order. Finding a word in the dictionary was a monumental task, as was organizing his work properly on paper. His handwriting was poor, nearly beyond recognition as understandable language. His thoughts often seemed disorganized and out of order. These are all functions of left hemispheric organization. While Bobby could organize such functions, he "naturally" tended to view information in a "holistic" manner, looking at the entirety of the information rather than at specific parts or at the logical order. With assistance though, he was able to organize and perform in appropriate ways if the adult understood that his was neither a learning disability nor a neurological dysfunction, but rather a different mode of thought process than that usually expected or required in the school and home situation. It has been our experience that most boys and girls like Bobby who display the cerebral dissonance syndrome need not have special education but can be easily assisted during the elementary years within the regular school curriculum. Unfortunately, many boys and girls are often misdiagnosed as learning disabled or as emotionally disordered, which subsequently generates inaccurate expectations in both teachers and parents resulting in difficulties for the child.

Children with the cerebral dissonance syndromes are children who, though they display at least low to high average ability in language function, tend to have much higher capabilities in the nonverbal or right hemispheric function, which is their major mode of consciousness and cognitive organization. Education and socialization are processes involving what may be called "left minded" cognitive organization. In this case, the functions of the left hemisphere are given the majority of stimulation through usual home or parent training. There is a high degree of stimulation and reward in school through reading, writing, spelling, mathematics, and behavioral expectations.

	Hemisphere Efficiency/IQ		Language Lateralization	Motor	Visual	Characteristics
	Right	Left				
I	100	100	Left	Right	Right	Assumed normal child, average learning and adjustment.
II	100	115 and above	Left	Right	Right or Left	Typically achievement-oriented child, does well in school including gifted with high verbal IQ. Potential frustration with written work, tendency to dislike unconventional and creative arts and learning.
III	115+	115+	Left	Right	Right or Left	Gifted child with high capacities in both hemispheres.
IV	90 or less	115+	Left	Left	Left or Right	Bright verbal child with ipsilateral left hemispheric control of left hand. Tendency toward directional and spatial confusion and frustration. Dislike of creative, artistic, athletic, and constructive activities. Poor writing skills.
V	115+	100	Left	Right	Right or Left	Creative child. Difficulty in spatial organization, disregard for social rules, impulsive, musically inclined or athletic, general dislike of school. Whole word reader. Poor writing skills. Ipsilateral control of right hand by right hemisphere. The Alpha Child.
VI	115+	90 or less	Right and Left	Left	Left	Highly nonverbal child, creative but poor perceptual motor development. Moody, difficulty with time, behavioral organization, difficulty in reading. Probable left hemisphere language dysfunction with poor lateralization. Pathological left-hander.
VII	115+	100	Right	Left	Left	Genetic left-hander. Creative, musical, artistic, athletic, fantasy-oriented, unconventional.

Figure 3: Examples of potential hemispheric organization patterns.

While the functions of the right hemisphere are utilized in these areas, right hemispheric activity, in this case, is primarily a supportive function to the dominance of left hemispheric activity. In school only certain activities, for example, art, music, physical education, woodworking and other manual arts, involve naturalistic thought as the major organization mode. Cerebral Dissonance Syndrome children can learn the usual language-based activities, but they are difficult and provide less personal reinforcement of naturalistic capacities, leaving the child feeling somehow incompetent, or as many such children tell us, "just plain dumb." This has the expected result of creating frustration and feelings of anger in the child which neither he nor the teacher understand since he "seems like a bright child." The syndrome does not produce an incompetent child but one who sees and understands the world about him in grossly different ways than do others.

In Bobby's case we also saw parental reactions which are not uncommon with these sorts of children. Often, either the mother or the father recognize, during testing of the child, some of the same problems they had as a child, and for the first time the parent also begins to understand why he, too, experienced difficulty in school. In this case, it was the father who stated that it appeared that he was not unlike his son when he was a boy. The father was a graduate chemist who, though he had great difficulty with reading had developed an intense interest in chemistry as a boy. He was a highly competent individual who enjoyed research work which involved much visual imagery and creative problem solving. Once the father had graduated and begun work as a chemist, he was able to utilize his highly capable right hemispheric visual imagery without the need to constantly explain ideas with words. He had never been very good with math but the sort of mathematical requirements he found in chemistry did not seem to be a problem. Our experience with adults suggests that, once the highly capable right-minded individual enters an occupational field where he can utilize his highest level of cognitive skills, as opposed to working so much with words as in school subjects like English and Literature, he begins to find that he is quite capable after all.

The important aspect of the cerebral dissonance syndrome is its potential distinctiveness from other behaviors which involve neurological dysfunction or emotional disturbance. Many of the normal behaviors of the cerebral dissonance syndrome individual do appear much like the characteristics of these developmental defects in other individuals. This makes for a complex diagnostic problem, for one must decide if an individual is disturbed, is neurologically incompetent, or is a hemispherically different individual. But even this problem offers exciting possibilities. Even if an individual does have left hemispheric damage but intact right hemispheric capacity, he may respond to the same approaches as the individual who is displaying the cerebral dissonance syndrome. In the case of the individual with some sort of left hemispheric difficulty, treatment will involve an intensification of the same approaches used with the cerebral dissonance syndrome individual. Certainly, the cerebral dissonance individual, with his intact but less competent left hemispheric capacity, will display more generalized capabilities than the individual with left hemispheric damage, but both will benefit from similar educational and parental approaches to behavior and learning.

Estimates of incidence of cerebral dissonance syndrome children would be difficult to assess, but our own work would suggest that these children are much more numerous in school populations than might be supposed. The difficulty in making such estimates is due to the probability that many cerebral dissonance children are not true genetically inclined individuals but, rather, culturally induced syndrome individuals. Further, it must be remembered that the concepts of the cerebral dissonance individual are still only theoretical, though there is much evidence and some scattered research. It bears repeating that our purpose is to develop an approach to working with different personalities and learning styles, not to claim the cerebral dissonance theory as an entirely research-based theory.

The cerebral dissonance theory, while neurologically based, does yield a general notion of learning and personality style which can be tested within the classroom. It has already had some classroom application, not so much as a neurological theory, but as a practical means of expanding the horizon in observation and understanding of child development. In such observations it is expected that the teacher will find several children in the school population who exhibit either blatant characteristics of the cerebral dissonance syndrome or at least many specific though less obvious characteristics.

Motor Dominance

There is a wealth of information concerning motoric and visual dominance which has been researched from many perspectives. The conflicting conclusions of this research tend to fog the issues about the cerebral dissonance syndrome. It was, in fact, these very concepts of visual and motoric dominance in relation to learning problems which originally led to the present formulation of the cerebral dissonance syndrome.

Motoric dominance is a developmental consequence of the establishment of adequate differentiation in the different parts of the body resulting in a sort of neurological midline which separates the left and right sides of the body. The young infant responds to general stimuli with what is called "undifferentiated" motoric responses which means that an infant, when startled, will respond with motor movements in both sides of the body at once without any specific or "undifferentiated" movements of one side or limb of the body. As soon as the young infant begins to use one limb or the other usually during the latter half of the first year, he begins to gain differential control over the specific parts of the body. This lays the basis for eventual locomotive function whereby one limb can be moved in counter function with another to propel the body either in a crawling or eventually walking motion. At this stage, elementary levels of motoric dominance are already being established in gross motor movements. The preference for beginning movement with one side or the other is now being established, although it may alternate for some time from one side to the other, so that, by the age of eighteen months, most children are using one foot to initiate movement on a somewhat regular basis or to use one hand in preference to the other. As the development of grasping movements gives way to more sophisticated finger dexterity, handedness also becomes established. This follows the establishment of gross motor preference and is a later sophistication of the same preference for one side of the body.

The arguments continue concerning the basis of establishing left- or right-handedness and are far from resolved in favor of a genetic cause, an environmental basis, or a combination. Our experience has led us to accept the conclusion that there is a strong genetic or, at least, prenatal determination in the establishment of motor dominance, but that there are a number of environmental factors which can intervene in this process. Sometimes, the naturally left-handed child may select the right hand for a number of cultural or even physical reasons without serious consequences to later motoric or learning competency. There are children who may select the left hand for similar reasons even though they may have a natural preference for the right.

An important point related to the development of motoric dominance *must* be recognized in order to understand the cerebral dissonance theory and the general problems in motoric dominance. The two hemispheres of the brain both develop control of the appropriate motor side through a natural sequence of learning. First the infant gains control of the neck and shoulders, next the general arm movements, then the lower arms, the wrists, and finally the hands and fingers. The infant begins to learn these movements during the first few days of life, but does not gain full control of hands and fingers until the period between the end of the third year and the beginning of the sixth. While there are great differences between individual children as to rate and sophistication of the process, it always occurs in normally developing children in this sequence.

For the teacher, an understanding of the stages of this process is very important. Equally important is the fact that a child develops motor control from the midline of the body out to the extremity. With the learning of these sequential movements, a significant neurological organization is created. The left hemi-spheric, right-handed child learns to control from the middle out or from left to right. The right hemispheric, left-handed child, learns from the middle out but this results in a right to left orientation. Now we can understand why the right-handed child writes from the left to the right and why the world is a motoric right-handed world. Letters are made from the left to the right when the right-handed child is working. For the left-handed child, great confusion occurs because there is a differ-ence between what the eyes tell him is there and what his hand reproduces. The left-handed child, seeing a lower case "b" will copy it into a lower case "d" because the motoric system of the left-handed child will make the letter in the natural way from right to left. So the left-handed child has to train himself to disregard the natural motor tendency to go right to left and move his hand, for him, in exactly the opposite way. He must, in other words, learn to write backwards. It is only through much practice that the child eventually is able to teach his motor cortex not to respond to visual imagery in a natural manner motorically. How long it takes the child to learn this "neurological switch" will depend on general language and intellectual capacities and on the amount of experience he gains.

It is most important that the teacher and parent realize that the left-handed child "naturally" makes letters from right to left because the right hemisphere developed motor control in a right to left sequence, from the midline out, just as the right-handed individual developed from the shoulder out to the hand in a left to right sequence. This sequence of development from the midline of the body out to the extremities seems to have profound mental organization effects not only on the develop-ment of motor organization but also on cognitive organization. Since the most usual organization in the culture is left to right, the left-handed child is said to write backwards or organize in a backward way. It must be understood that this notion of "back-wards" is a cultural value and not a neurological reality. The left-handed, right to left organization, is as natural and appro-priate neurologically as is the cultural norm structure of left to right. The left-handed individual is simply different from the norm. If, by some genetic and evolutionary condition, the right to left organization had become the norm, and there is some evidence suggesting man was not always a right-handed creature, then all right-handers would be said to "write backwards."

The left-handed world should not be considered an accident of nature but a neurological choice which is dependent on both genetic or prenatal conditions and on the cultural environment. The hemispheres of the brain demonstrate tremendous ability and flexibility, and regardless of a natural tendency toward one mode of organization or the other, it is possible for either hemisphere to assume dominance in hand preference. The left-handed or "right-minded" individual is organized in as efficient a manner as is the right-handed or "left-minded" individual. The task for the left-handed child is to adapt his organization into a world that is dominated by individuals with the opposite mode of organization.

In Figure 4 a simplified drawing of basic neurological organization is illustrated. There are three major features of this structure which are essential to our discussion. First, the motor cortex in each hemisphere controls and directs motor behavior on the opposite side of the body. Second, each hemisphere develops sequential control of motoric responses from the neurological midline to the extremity of the body. Because this control is learned in sequence, a particular mental organization develops. Finally the visual input from each eye is also crossed over the midline of the body so that each eye supplies one-half of the visual input to each hemisphere.

The interrelationships between motor dominance, visual input, and visual kinesthetic feedback are illustrated in Figure 5. Many teachers believe that light from each eye goes to one or the other visual cortex. This is not true in that visual information from both eyes is split into two channels leading to each eye. In this way half of the visual input from each eye goes to each hemisphere's visual cortex. Light coming into the eye from the right of the body or the visual field strikes the left side of each eye or retina. In this way light from the right side is

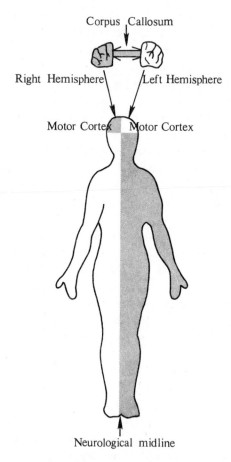

Corpus Callosum

Right Hemisphere   Left Hemisphere

Motor Cortex   Motor Cortex

Neurological midline

Figure 4: Illustration of the neurological crossover in motor control and reception of kinesthetic feedback. Left hemisphere motor cortex receives tactile and kinesthetic information from right side of the body. The motor cortex in this hemisphere controls and directs muscle function on the right side of the body. The interhemispheric connection between the two hemispheres provides a constant flow of information between the two hemispheres as to the activity of the other.

channeled, by each eye, to the left hemisphere. Light then is channeled into the hemisphere on the side of the eye which receives it. Fortunately, this provides the maximum amount of visual information to the hemisphere which motorically controls the hand on the side of the body from where the light came. The converse is true for the left side of the body or light coming from the left side of the body or the left visual field. This light strikes the right side of the retina and is channeled to

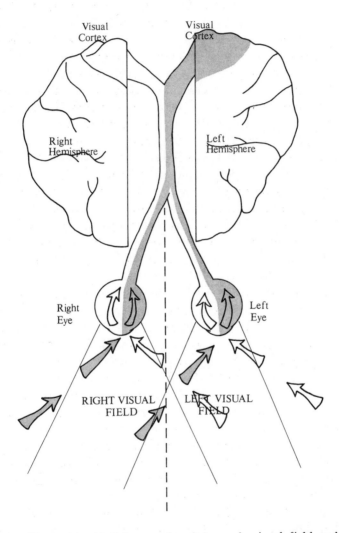

Figure 5: Illustration of light entering from each visual field and being transmitted to opposite visual cortex. Light entering from right visual field strikes left half of each eye and is transmitted to left hemisphere which controls motoric function on the right side of the body or from the visual field in origin of visual information.

the right visual-motor system.

As the light is channeled from the right side of the body to the left hemisphere, that visual information is available for control and manipulation of the right hand and right side of the body. As the movement is executed, visual and kinesthetic information from that side of the body provides feedback as to the effectiveness of the motor execution of movement. This feedback allows for rapid change and correction of movement.

This organization provides an efficient motor response of using one hand or the other. In times of danger, for instance, if information from the eyes were not sent to the coordinating motor hemisphere, then we would be less capable of responding rapidly to the unexpected movement of objects coming from one side or the other. Further, in learning and coordinating body movements, it is important that visual information from the right side be forwarded, in as complete a form as possible, to the hemisphere that controls that side of the body. We do not have to consciously watch ourselves walk, but the visual and motor areas of the brain are doing just that without our conscious awareness.

Establishment of one side as the dominant motor area is an important developmental milestone. Regardless of which side of the body becomes the dominant motor area, one side must develop this facility or we would be unable to learn to walk, to move in coordinated ways, or to make the many directional decisions needed to effectively alter our motor behavior. Imagine the confusion we would experience if every time we started to take a step both sides of the body moved at the same time. The child who establishes motor dominance late often experiences much confusion and general clumsiness because each movement must be consciously considered so that one side or the other is used as the leader or initiator of movement. As we have stated, dominance tendency and handedness apparently begins as early as the first year and should be somewhat established by the third year. The importance of motor dominance and organization reaches far beyond the simple notion of motor control and movement. In the following discussion we will consider some of the ramifications when this process does not proceed normally.

Visual-Motor Dominance

There has been much discussion in recent years about children who do not display visual-motor dominance in the usual manner. In most classrooms approximately 20 to 30 percent of the children may not exhibit clearly defined visual-motor dominance. Usually, just as in the case of motor dominance with the hands and legs, one dominant eye leads the nondominant eye in the initiation of visual movement. One eye, usually the one on the dominant motor side of the body, is used to select a target while the nondominant eye converges to fixate on the same target selected by the dominant eye. Thus, when a child is attempting to converge on a visual target such as a moving ball or a letter on the page of a reader, one eye converges on the object while the nondominant eye follows to become fixated along with the dominant eye on the target. This skill of eye movement matures slowly and becomes more sophisticated as the child gains practice in fine visual and motor movements. The rate of maturation in this particular skill varies tremendously between children, but most are fairly proficient by the age of seven years. Just as when aiming a gun at a target, the child finds more ease in writing if he uses the eye on the dominant motor side of his body as the dominant eye.

There are many children who not only mature late in visual-motor coordination but many do not use the eye on the dominant motor side as their dominant eye. Some children are left-eyed and right-handed or right-eyed and left-handed. This is usually referred to as "cross dominance or mixed dominance," and for some time teachers have suspected this as a cause of various learning problems including reversals of letters or poor writing skills. Our experience has not supported this notion though many of these children do have learning problems. Most often there will be as many cross dominant children in the upper reading or achievement groups as will be found in groups of poorly achieving children.

Since the cross dominance factor has not demonstrated any sort of consistent relationship to learning difficulties, we felt that additional factors must be operating. The major factor which did seem to complicate cross dominance was how well the child had established general balance and "kinesthetic feed-back" with subsequent motor coordination. Kinesthetic refers to "sensitivity and awareness of feedback from the activity and stress of muscle movement." How well the child is able to "feel" the subtle stresses of muscle movement during balance determines how quickly he can right himself or maintain efficient balance. Cross dominant children without kinesthetic problems did not seem to have as much difficulty adjusting to the cross dominant factor as children who did have poor kinesthetic skills.

As the young child develops control of his body and differentiates the sides and parts of the body through kinesthetic feedback he gains ever-increasing efficiency in movement. This is a feedback mechanism of the central nervous system. The child moves and receives constant internal information in the motor cortex concerning the appropriateness of his movement. In this manner he can alter movements in a rapid and efficient manner.

Several factors can delay or impair a child's ability to receive and process kinesthetic information. If the child has a poorly developed musculature system, the rate at which he develops effective balance may be delayed. Children with nutritional deficiencies or with a variety of metabolic dysfunctions may display impaired motor development which, in turn, delays the development of effective motor kinesthetic feedback. The child who is not allowed to explore or who has sparse experience in motor behavior during the early years may suffer from balance difficulties. Temporary illness or physical disabilities also play a role in preventing the child from practicing motor behavior at critical periods of development. It should be obvious that cerebral dysfunction may also impair such development.

While all of the foregoing factors contribute to poor balance, there are additional and more complex factors which may play a role. Most of the foregoing conditions are somewhat well known and have appeared in medical and educational literature for some time. But the cerebral dissonance child often has such difficulties, and it is here that a more advanced notion of dominance theory must be reviewed.

Too often in observing the learning and developmental behavior of children there is an overemphasis on the notion of visual and motor dominance. This is because the concept of cerebral dominance is not generally recognized, particularly in relation to visual and motor dominance. While there may be a significant relationship between visual dominance and learning or organizational behaviors, most often it appears that motor dominance and kinesthetic abilities are the determining factors. The child appears to be able to adjust to either left or right visual dominance, regardless of motor preference, if kinesthetic capabilities are intact. It would appear that motor dominance and kinesthetic abilities play a significant role in the child's learning adaptive abilities. The teacher and parent should understand these factors in order to assist the left-handed child who is having difficulties in directional orientation.

Cerebral Dominance

While a child usually establishes cerebral dominance in the same hemisphere as motor dominance, it is our feeling that this is not always true. Cerebral dominance, as has been discussed, is most often established in the left hemisphere due to general genetic effects or a combination of genetic and cultural training. Certainly, there is a significant emphasis given to socialized, left hemispheric development by the culture which must have a significant role in forcing utilization of socialized dominance in the left hemisphere.

Cerebral dominance, if it is a viable concept, would suggest tremendous implications for personality and learning. As has been discussed, an individual may, due to genetic and environmental reasons, develop a cerebral dominance in naturalistic thought organization over that of socialized thought. Such an individual would display many deviant personality and learning characteristics in that he may tend to be more natural-istic, have difficulty with time and sequence, language, and values.) This was assumed to be the case with Bobby cited in the previous discussion. (Because Bobby displayed much higher function in nonverbal or naturalistic thought than in verbal thought, it would appear that his dominant mode of conscious-ness was that of the right hemisphere.) This is why we call children like Bobby, Alpha children, for they tend to demon-strate all of the characteristics of right hemispheric dominance. If Bobby were truly a right hemispheric child and if motor and cerebral dominance were the same function, then Bobby would have been a left-handed child, *but Bobby was a right-handed child.* Not all children who are naturalistic thinkers are left-handed. Further, in our experience, not all left-handed children are naturalistic thinkers. It has been demonstrated again and again that there appears to be a general tendency toward con-sonant hemispheric dominance and handedness or motoric dominance but this is not by any means fixed. This single factor is a significant development in understanding the nature of thought organization and personality orientation. It may well be that many children who are seen as learning disabled, hyperactive, or distractable are children who may have disson-ance between motoric and cerebral dominance. It is not sup-posed that most children who are hyperactive or learning disabled are children with the cerebral dissonance syndrome but it is suggested that many such children are in fact special sorts of children, the Alpha children. One of the major existing problems is that the adaptive abilities of higher species are so well developed that they may actually work to the natural child's detriment. For example, he goes undetected if he is able to overcome his natural tendency to organize from right to left.)

In our culture, if a child does have a difference in cerebral capacities between the two forms of organization, the difference is less critical when the socialized mode of thought is dominant since this is the mode which is required in so much formal learning. But if a child is a naturalistic thinker who utilizes the right hemisphere as the dominant mode then this child will have many difficulties. It is assumed that most children develop so-called "normal" cerebral potentiality in which both forms of thought are more or less equalized. But some review of early childhood environments would suggest that probability is far from the actual reality. For example, in poorly socialized or deprived environments we would expect that socialized thought organization would receive less stimulation during the early years than motoric and naturalistic behavior simply because language and values, appropriate to learning in the schools, are not so stringently reinforced as in the middle or upper class. However, either socialized or naturalistic modes of thought may be culturally induced in families where certain kinds of social environments are dominant. It may be possible, as has been suggested, that the combination of genetics and environmental conditioning in the most critical years of early childhood are a major determinant of cerebral dominance. Realizing that the earliest training of a child has the most impact on neurological development, we must realize the possibility that Alpha children may be produced by the culture in numbers far greater than one might expect.

Suppose for a minute that we accept the notion that usually a child will develop a consonant motoric dominance organization in which the dominant hemisphere is the same as that of later hand dominance. This would mean that most right-handed children would be "left-minded," and if there were a difference in hemispheric capacities, the right hemisphere would be the less endowed. Conversely, if the child is left-handed we would expect a right hemispheric mode of thought organization or "right-mindedness." If both hemispheres were somewhat equally competent, then, "right-mindedness" would not be a handicap, for the child could learn appropriate language and cultural values even though there would be a tendency toward naturalistic thought.

Handedness, Genetics, and the Alpha Child

Many contemporary researchers have disclaimed any evidence

that there is a genetic basis for handedness. Yet, the general tendency of neurological research today is to accept a somewhat strong viewpoint in favor of genetic influence on handedness. A majority of premature neonates (28 weeks post-conception) show a rightward tonic neck reflex. The direction of the reflex at birth and hand preference at age ten is significantly correlated (Gesell and Ames, 1947),[1] while a strong, though imperfect, correlation exists between cerebral dominance and handedness in a study done by Goodglass and Quadfasal in 1954.[1] This would seem to indicate that handedness is largely determined genetically; however, this in turn is not a significant determiner of cerebral dominance. Dimond[1] states "it appears therefore, that while lateral preferences in nonhuman animals result from accidental contingencies of reinforcement, those in human beings and in their humanoid ancestors are expressions of a predisposing genotype."[1]

It would appear that there is a strong genetic predisposition toward right-handedness and left hemispheric dominance. In left-handed individuals, language may be less well lateralized, resulting in a more diffused system of language control and function between the two hemispheres. It has been postulated that such diffusion may result in a diminishing of general spatial-motor capacity, and this was borne out in a 1969 study by Levy.[1] It has been shown by Reitan (1955)[1] and Arrigoni and DeRenze (1964) that the Wechsler Adult Intelligence Scale (W.A.I.S.) measures verbal and perceptual function. Using the W.A.I.S. with selected Caltech students, Levy found that sinistrals did display a significantly lower performance or perceptual function score in comparison to their language scores than did dextrals. Other studies have reported similar findings.

Studies concerning left-handed or right-handed individuals often display a relationship between handedness and cerebral dominance. In many left-handed individuals the poor lateralization of language and difficulties in spatial motor functions is well known. Yet, in our work it has not been this particular phenomenon which concerned us. It was, rather, a completely different way of looking at children who had learning and/or behavioral difficulties. Miller (1971) gave both verbal and perceptual tests to sinistral and dextral university students and confirmed Levy's initial finding. The two groups did not differ on the verbal tests, but the left-handed students were inferior on the perceptual tests.[1] It has been suggested by some researchers that left-handed people have two left hemispheres. A study completed at the University of Texas (reported by Dimond[1]) in 1971 found that sinistrals constituted 11 percent of the student population at the University of Texas, but only 6 percent of art students and 18 percent of law students. In a survey of mathematics departments in a number of universities, there were no left-handed topologists. Quinan (1922) found that among one hundred musicians, sixteen were sinistral, while among one hundred machinists, only four were left-handed.[1] Dimond[1] suggests that the possession of two left hemispheres improves those skills dependent on the left hemisphere relative to the performance achieved by a single, fully lateralized left hemisphere. Lateral specialization does not optimize each set of capabilities individually, but optimizes some joint function sets. The laterally specialized person is, in this sense, a generalist, while the laterally nonspecialized person is a specialist.[1]

This research suggests that in the truly left-handed person, speech and language centers tend to be less lateralized and exist in both hemispheres and that there may be certain advantages in some language areas over the dextral but a loss of lateralized abilities in spatial skills. We have found, however, that there is another approach to questions of handedness and cerebral dominance. In most of the studies cited here, there was concern for the effects of poorly lateralized hemispheric function on spatial abilities or language. The subjects which were the concern of most studies were either left-handed individuals or individuals with some sort of brain dysfunction or abnormality. *Sperry's work in 1969 and Gazzaniga's, Bogen's, and Sperry's in 1967 have shown a most important but overlooked possibility that voluntary movement of not only the left but the right-hand can be initiated by the right cerebral hemisphere.*[2,3] It would seem implausible that initiating voluntary movement is the prerogative of the dominant hemisphere and that it alone issues "command signals" to muscular action. It is exactly this phenomenon which finally led the authors to look upon left- and right-handedness in a very different way.

We have seen many children demonstrating poorly lateralized function who, like those in the studies cited here, were assumed to be left-handed or who had some sort of brain dysfunction. But we have seen many children who did not display the typical signs of difficulties experienced by left-handers. For example, many left-handed children appear to have little difficulty with letter reversals, poor spatial organization, "two left hemispheres" resulting in higher language function than spatial, or many of the difficulties often presented by left-handers in spatial or motoric work such as cited above. Further, and most importantly, we have found many children among the learning disabled who, though right-handed, appeared to have many of the typical difficulties of the left-handed child. These were not children who had been "forced" into right-handed orientation by parents who found them to be favoring the left-hand. Our final analysis suggested that for some reason we were seeing children who, *though right-handed, appeared to be controlling that hand with the right hemisphere organization.* An additional element was that on the W.I.S.C. these children demonstrated higher performance scores than verbal scores, though their verbal scores were within the average range or above. This suggested to us the possibility that some children, both left- and right-handed, tended to have a predominantly right hemispheric organization and motor control emanating. These are not findings which would become evident from research studies where the researchers were looking for cerebral dysfunction or a difference between right- and left-handed children. It is our belief that such researchers, because they are primarily psychologists or neurologists, did not have the sort of day-to-day contact with children that would bring them to look at their data from this viewpoint. If, as a researcher, one is oriented toward a particular clinical viewpoint, that viewpoint tends to discriminate among the criteria and data to fit the model under study. Since much of the research is accomplished in a typically "left minded" and logical orientation, it is unlikely that a more creative and flexible viewpoint might emerge. In essence, we feel that much of the hemispheric research is so organized upon left minded viewpoint that little can be learned which does not clinically fit a preconceived model of left hemispheric function as being the dominant hemisphere and the right being the minor. All conclusions and study appear to be based on that assumption.

In studies on left-handedness there was no attempt to look at behavior over a broad range of factors including reading and school achievement, creativity, intuitiveness, personality factors, and general personal organization. There, obviously, were no studies in the literature that could be found looking for right-handed individuals who appeared to demonstrate "right minded" or right hemispheric organization. In essence, most of the reported research is too narrow and limited to gain a truly comprehensive understanding of the full range of factors involved in left- and right-handedness or the relationship of handedness and cerebral dominance. The simple notion that the preference of a hand suggests the dominant hemisphere is, at this point, too primitive to provide much understanding of learning and personality structure, as well. Our own early theory has yet to be bolstered by a respectable amount of study, but it is advanced for the purpose of assisting teachers and parents in looking in a new way at the behavior of their children. The following assumptions have emerged from our own work and study of several hundred children with learning and behavior problems.

> There are at least three major areas of neurological function relative to cerebral dominance which must be accounted for in understanding a child's learning and behavioral characteristics.
> a. Motoric dominance
> b. Cerebral dominance in cognitive organization
> c. Cerebral capacity and efficiency

After approximately the age of five to six years, a number of tests and observations can be used to determine handedness of a child. Many children at this age have not established clear motoric dominance and certainly, along with other factors, there may be clear evidence of poor lateralization. But in most cases other than those demonstrating some clear evidence of pathology, a child will demonstrate preference and efficiency in motoric function with one hand or the other. If the child is left-handed, motorically, there will be some difficulty in adjusting to a right-handed or left-to-right organized world. If the child is right-handed, it would be assumed that there will be no great difficulty in orienting in a left-to-right fashion. Dependent upon cerebral dominance, neither case may be true. While a child may select one hand or the other as a preferred hand, this does not imply actual left- or right-handedness even though the preferred hand is that one which the child motorically demonstrates the most efficient management. The first question to resolve is which hand the child prefers and is most competent with.

The second is to determine if the child's general behavioral characteristics appear consonant with the selected hand. This is more difficult, but many indicators do exist in the classroom or through daily learning and social behavior. These factors, of course, are not usually available to the clinical researcher since he is unable to be with the child enough to gain such information. Such a study would be quite time-consuming but is possible through continuing work with teachers and parents.

Children who demonstrate adequate language skills and who are left-handed may exhibit no difficulties in spatial organization but actually demonstrate superior capabilities in motoric function. For example, many artists and musicians are left-handed as were many of the outstanding artists and musicians in history. It is our suggestion that these incongruities between the research cited previously and these outstanding individuals may have been due to the fact that these left-handers, as with many of the children we see, do not have poorly lateralized speech but are hemispherically lateralized in the usual fashion. The reason for this is that these are individuals who have adequate lateralization but a preference for the right hemispheric mode. They have more efficient operation and capacity in spatial creative functions and, in fact, are right hemispheric dominant, though there are no great difficulties in left hemispheric function. This, within neurological research, is very difficult to understand due to the dogmatic belief that the left hemisphere is the major hemisphere and the right is the minor hemisphere. Conversely, a left-handed individual may be a great debator and speaker, i.e. evidence left hemispheric dominance, but have adequate capacities in the right hemisphere also. In essence, we have seen many left-handed children and adults who did not demonstrate deficits in either language or spatial-creative functions. It is the relationship which is important and which hemisphere is actually dominant. But the simple notion of handedness as related to the dominant hemisphere is too simple to understand these individuals.

There are children who, though right-handed, demonstrate adequate speech and language skills or development but, like the case just cited, higher performance on spatial-creative abilities. Again, we often find that these are children who, though linguistically capable, seem to prefer spatial-creative functions like an individual who is right hemispheric dominant. They usually provide a significant amount of data which somewhat verifies right hemispheric dominance.

The important point here is that, though there are individuals who demonstrated poor lateralization who are left-handed, there are also other individuals who do not present poor lateralization but who still prefer naturalistic or right hemispheric control of their behavior. It is with these individuals that the notion that consciousness exists only in the "major" or left hemisphere comes to be somewhat absurd. In a later discussion we will touch upon the behavior of athletes, artists, and surgeons who must demonstrate high degrees of consciousness through right hemispheric expression but who are able to modulate their behavior and switch that consciousness to the verbal or left hemisphere.

Thus, the second question, that of hemispheric dominance, appears too complex to be resolved on the basis of existing research. In Chapter 6 a range of experimental neurological and behavioral factors are presented concerning assignment of hemispheric dominance in behavior and learning.

The final factor which complicates the research even more is that of hemispheric capacity. Capacity here implies that the hemisphere has some measureable level of efficiency. This can be done, though IQ tests or other measures of competence are suspect, through a variety of verbal and nonverbal tests and activities. The research previously cited used both the W.I.S.C. and the W.A.I.S. as indicators of left and right hemispheric capacity or efficiency with verbal and performance tests respectively. While there are other acceptable measures, these two tests are adequate to demonstrate our point here. We have found many children who demonstrate higher performance scores, though language scores might also be high. For example, children are often found who demonstrate performance scores in a range from 120 to above but with a verbal level of 100 to 110. Taken by themselves these differences mean little. But when one finds a child who enjoys spatial-creative tasks and who demonstrates excellent artistic, athletic, and/or musical ability while showing average ability in verbal activities, we suspect that not only is the right hemisphere the major hemisphere but that it is also more efficient. These children may be left- or right-handed, though in most cases right-handed, and are right minded individuals who appear to view their world in a characteristically right minded way even while they are able to function in the usual fashion of the left hemisphere activity. The individual child has no pathological abnormalities and no distinct learning disabilities; he is merely organized neurologically in a different manner. We call him an Alpha child.

In Chapter 6 we will spend some time investigating ways of identifying such children and the consequences of such organization. If we can assist the reader in understanding the phenomenon, then we may free many children and adults from the educational and psychological chains which have been placed on them in the form of labels like "learning disabled" and "emotionally disturbed" that are used by the "left minded" to explain what they do not and, due to their orientation, cannot understand. It will not be easy to separate these children from those who do have real left-handed pathology or emotional disturbance but it must be attempted.

The concept of the Alpha child should have important ramifications for education and upon educational curriculum which stresses mostly socialized and left minded learning but also naturalized and right minded learning. Such an equal emphasis must be made if we are to help those children with differences, as well as to provide for all children a program that will develop their full natural and socialized personalities.

On the practical side, the classroom teacher or parent may ask "But how can the adult tell which learning style is manifest in a particular child's behavior?" In response, it must be restated that there are no patterns of behavior which can be simply "diagnosed" and classified. Rather, in learning and development we are never dealing with the simple process of diagnosis and treatment. This is exactly the concept which our discussion here is intended to negate. If a child has the measles we can treat him; if he has a broken leg we can splint it; if he has a visual problem proper vision care and supervision can provide correction. When we discuss the brain, with the endless potentialities of the nervous system and its function in relation to the complex environment within which it learns, we are never dealing with absolutes, with definite cause-and-effect relationships. Understanding a child's needs requires recognition of the potential ways in which he may respond to any specific environmental or internal function. We must deal with possibilities, tentative hypothesis, and inferences from observable behavior. We must outline a basic premise concerning the child's needs based on these inferences and on a general knowledge of how the central nervous system functions and then proceed with educational processes that appear the most logical. As we proceed, the child's behavior and responses will provide a continuous feedback of information concerning his behavior and development. Based on such information, we can then test our hypothesis, and development of new strategies can occur. The present chapter gives us tentative theoretical concepts upon which we can build testable hypothesis for our work with children. In the coming chapters we will apply these theories to various aspects of learning which can be applied, in turn, to the classroom.

Chapter 4

THE LEARNING CHILD

THE child has one great task, to become a whole being. This task, begun quietly long before birth, is never complete, never total in the space of a human life. From the first year of struggle with uncontrolled limbs and with neurological organization to the adult years of fully functioning capacity, the individual must search not only his own being but the expanse of physical and social environment which becomes his world. This great adventure includes decisions about values, about the meaning and purpose of life, and an increasing awareness of language, culture, and personal meaning.

We as individuals can never return to childhood and the naturalistic fantasies of freedom without responsibility, yet we cannot lose this vital aspect of ourselves by immersion in only social meaning and values. Each of us is at once caught in our role of social responsibility and yet yearning for the happiness and joy of freedom from constant social evaluation. The task of teachers and parents is to give the opportunity for each individual to seek his own direction but with the skills of the culture whereby the search will be given reason and purpose.

It is not the natural child or the socialized child who finds full awareness in adulthood. It is the child who uses both of these capacities to become an integrated and complex being capable of understanding both human behavior and the natural world. The poet gives breath to fantasies and feelings deep within us but the philosopher gives these feelings reason and purpose. If we are to be both poet and philosopher, we must learn the skills of the culture, capture the language, and understand the order of things. To truly find our souls and the goal of our flight into tomorrow, time and space must become one. The human soul is universal meaning searching for an hour, a moment, in which to reflect and predict, to look ahead and back, to know our place not only in space but in time. There is no way presently known in which both the purposes of time and space can be melded except in integration of our naturalistic and socialized being. We can be neither poet nor philosopher; we must be both. Space and feeling are the world of our naturalistic being, and time and order are the substance of our socialized self. When we become parents and when we teach children, we are accepting the awesome task of giving another being the chance for personal fulfillment, but the choice to learn or to be must remain with the child. This task requires that we as parents and teachers learn as much as possible about the duality of being, the natural and social realms of human behavior and how they develop in consonant ways toward integration of the being.

The naturalistic aspect of being is based within the physiology of the central nervous system, in movement, and in the sensory world within ourselves. Socialization and formal learning give purpose and order to this complex world of naturalness. Without order, reason, language, and culture ours would be a world caught in space without yesterdays and tomorrows, faced with the constant challenge of the moment without recourse to organized and purposeful behavior except to fill our bellies and to reproduce our kind. The artist can capture his feeling, a still world, or hope upon his canvas but he cannot give it value to others without language and history. At the same time, history and destiny would be undefinable words without images and sensory experience. So it is that the child's task is giving purpose and order to his feelings and behavior if he is to truly find a place, a purpose, for his ceaseless wanderings and effort. Without order and purpose, Alpha children are caught in space without dimensions. They must live in a world without time unless a teacher or a parent can reach out to them. There are many shadings of naturalistic and socialized thought or cognitive organization and integrative function.

Cognitive and "cognitive learning" have become significant concepts in today's education. At the neurological level, the study of the psychoneurological aspects of learning and/or cognition become quite complex and beyond our discussion here, but a practical knowledge of behaviorally related theories of "thought," "cognition," or "learning" should be included in the training of each classroom teacher. The reader is referred to the many excellent texts listed in the chapter references for a more thorough study of cognitive theory. Here we wish to briefly inform the reader of several important concepts concerning cognitive function, particularly in their relation to right and left mindedness.

Cognition may be thought of as those processes of higher brain function in informational memory, processing, and expression which allow the child to learn symbolic language, categorize, store, and evaluate information, and to engage in problem solving and creative behaviors. This is a rather lengthy definition but it is essential that the teacher understand that, just as there are increasingly specialized levels of central nervous system function, so are there more and more complex behavioral response potentialities as a consequence of learning and higher brain function. For example, we have pointed out that at the time information enters the central nervous system, sensory data is received as sensation which activates neuronic potential but must be further processed in order for the individual to gain some awareness or recognition of the event. The second level includes perception or awareness and orientation of the incoming information.

The child may respond to the environment as a consequence of both sensations and perceptions but the nature of the responses may differ greatly in quality. For example, the anticipation of pain may be adequate stimulus for a physical response prior to the actual perception of pain. Perception involves a slightly more complex reaction in that the individual becomes "aware" of the sensation and responds to it in a more or less conscious manner, though the response may still be a reflex action. Perception may become more complex in that awareness of a particular sensation may stimulate perceptual or conscious awareness of the sensation and also require some sort of specially learned response. For example, the teacher may sense, at a precognitive level, that there is smoke in the room but the sensation is not sufficient to cause a conscious or perceptual awareness. Eventually the smoke sensation breaks through to the conscious level of awareness, at which time the teacher, rather than taking flight like a frightened animal, seeks additional information from the environment, a cognitive function, upon which she can make a decision about the danger involved and the source or nature of the smoke. Following this higher level of perception and evaluation, she then responds in an appropriate manner.

In the foregoing example we see the three major levels of central nervous system response: sensation, perceptual awareness, and cognitive evaluation. Perceptual awareness can include only minor or low level awareness of an event or it can become involved in higher level perception and cognition. "Perception," in our use here, refers to that intermediate level of central nervous system function between the lower brain centers where sensations are first received, and the higher brain centers where that sensation becomes embued with some sort of meaning through higher brain stem activity or cortical involvement. This is an example also of the difference between reflex or unmediated responses and mediated responses. Mediation is the transmission of sensations to the brain stem from the lower centers where the sensation is altered into perceptual awareness ready for some sort of *decision-making* function by the higher brain centers. This decision-making capacity, which is present to some degree in many lower animals, is much more sophisticated and complex in higher animals and man.

Cognitive function is dependent upon the abilities of the higher brain mechanism and automatic sensory motor mechanism along with the interpretive cortex, prefrontal lobes, and associated tissues which involve memory, foresight, and present-past synthesis of information toward problem-solving skills. These brain functions provide, for man, extensive ability to mediate and evaluate perceptual information and to develop novel or unique responses which meet the demands of the situation. This results in the flexible and adaptive ability of man to learn new ways to survive in his environment. Man must learn cognitive skills and as a consequence develop adaptive behaviors. Cognitive development relies on the existence of uncommitted areas of the brain tissue and the ability to program them in behavioral potentialities, and the ability to alter behavior continually to meet ever-changing environmental conditions.

In addition to the above definition, cognition must also be described differently relative to right and left mindedness. Too often, authors discuss cognition as a process which involves language learning, rational behavior, and the more formalized learning found in the classrooms. This may be an inadequate model for understanding cognitive behavior and also has dangerous implication for the education of children. If cognition is primarily associated with language, i.e. left mindedness, then formal education may fail to provide the balanced setting necessary for the development of both right and left mindedness. Our model of cognition function must be broadened to include both hemispheres.

Left minded learning, cognition, requires the use of abstract language symbols which represent reality in the processing of information. Information about time, sequence, and social values is used to formulate or to develop specific behavioral response potentialities. Thus, by using factual data, the individual can reason his way toward certain assumptions about his behavior and the condition of his environment. We understand this information to be more or less objective if it is based on fact. This is the usual belief about the role of cognition in formal learning. But what of the right hemisphere?

The right hemisphere with its capacities to synthesize and integrate information in a holistic manner provides consciousness with more flexibility than would be achieved by relying upon the factual and well-organized capacities of the left hemisphere. Because of its synthesizing ability, the right hemisphere provides an extended and important function for conscious use of perceptual information. When the individual is engaged in socialized thought, the left hemisphere provides the major portion of information processing ability with the right hemisphere playing a supportive role in the cognitive act. But is a reverse role possible? Can cognition rely primarily on right hemispheric function with the left providing a supportive role? One need only watch the artist, the surgeon, or the carpenter to discover the answer. When man engages in nonverbal cognition, the left hemisphere provides that amount of order or reason, memory or logic, and decision making needed to support the nonverbal cognitive function. For example, an individual attempting to design, in his mind, a house or building is able to use categorized structural information which is spatial in nature to create a new and unique structure. He may utilize certain rules of social meaning and value in making his mental structure, but the cognitive activity is essentially a visualization of images which have not heretofore existed. He can appraise his creation relative to energy use, protection from the elements, beauty, and practicality, all without extensive verbal, cognitive skills. If we continue this example we can imagine all sorts of cognitive functions which do not rely on language-based cognition. Thus, an individual, even without extensive verbal, cognitive skills, can think in critical ways and perform most of the important activities now usually ascribed only to the left hemispheric based cognition.

Recognition of the importance of nonverbal cognitive abilities can make a significant change in much of the educational theory about how children learn, and it certainly can have the impact of increasing our effectiveness in providing a holistically based curriculum for children and the development of their full potential.

As the discussion proceeds in coming chapters, much attention will be given to the problem of developing full range cognitive abilities in children and how current techniques in education tend to ignore this important aspect of hemisphericity and to inadvertently inhibit the growth we intend for our children.

An associated concept which is currently popular in learning theory is that of "affective" function. In many educational programs we find "cognitive and affectual" education as a primary curriculum focus. Our brief encounter with the concept of cognition should include, at this point, some definition of "affective." Affective refers to "feeling," to emotions, and to the subjective aspect of consciousness. Education and learning today have expanded this meaning and given it a distinctive and specific meaning. Our task is to distinguish between the original meaning, the currently popular educational meaning, and the neurological correlates of the function.

In education the concept of affective development includes basic perceptual awareness of the situation or environment, willingness to attend to or to receive information about the environment, and selective attention to specific aspects of the environment.[1] Affective implies that the individual is not evaluating or emotionally responding but merely responding at the voluntary level of awareness. For our purposes here, the initial level of awareness must be described as being a result of both right and left hemispheric function. If the situation involves a social group or a forest scene, the individual is responding to either the spatial and sensory aspects of the environment or to actual verbal input. Thus, depending upon the stimulus, the child may respond to only language-based information or to spatial sensory information or, in many situations, to both forms of information at the same time.

The next level of affective function is a conscious decision and response. The individual makes "a decision" to respond either in a passive or active manner. The child may listen to the teacher passively or he may respond with a question or an answer. In either case he has decided to make the response. At this level some cognition is, of course, involved and he leaves the realm of mere affective behavior. But the essential characteristic here is that the child responds because he "feels," i.e. is personally motivated to respond. His response is one that is primarily affective. Next the child makes some sort of social or personal value decision concerning the situation. This means that he holds some sort of belief or "preference" for responding or not responding. This again may be based on social values or it may be based on personal "feelings." For example, the child may respond to the teacher because he believes it is expected of him, or he may respond for reasons of personal interest in the situation, because he "likes" the teacher or feels good about her, or because he enjoys the involvement with another human being at the feeling or emotional level. These responses exhibit some sort of "value" which motivates the child into his behavior. It is important here to recognize that there is a difference between affective behavior which includes either social or personal values. Too often in value education, the emphasis has been placed on social values rather than on internal or emotional values. A value can be either social or personal and, through cognition in either hemisphere, change to another. For example, a child may enjoy running for the sheer physical and emotional pleasure it brings. This is a right minded motivation and one that more clearly fits the affective emotional definition. But as the child learns to run he may also learn that it is fun to win in races because of the praise and attention it brings. In this case, running, originally a personal, affective value, becomes a social value held for the sake of competition and social recognition.

At higher levels of value or affective learning the individual continues to develop systems of values which are both social and personal. The individual may develop extensive belief systems concerning social behavior, social interaction, and personal values such as a strong belief in the preservation of nature or religious preferences. At these higher levels the capacities of both left and right hemispheric function, naturalistic and socialized, become more and more intertwined, making for extensive belief and value systems that integrate both social beliefs and personal values.

Naturalistic Cognitive Function

Our naturalistic tendency in perception and cognitive function is to organize information into a "gestalt" or to see the entirety of a thing, a thought, or a feeling as opposed to looking at individual parts as in socialized and evaluative thought. This naturalistic and total response tendency is most closely attuned to the senses such as smell, taste, touch, sound in the form of nonverbal or musical activity, and, most importantly, feelings or emotion. Thoughts can come rushing in upon our naturalistic mind that are emotionally overwhelming, totally absorbing, and highly fulfilling. There are not words, we often say, to explain how we *feel*. This is the world of high psychic and mystical awareness. When we are totally in love, when a musical score brings ecstacy, when we come to feel a oneness with nature, or when we are suddenly aware of the meaning of God, these are naturalistic and highly sensory thoughts which exist beyond social evaluation and words.

The naturalistic mode of consciousness is a most basic level of human awareness which brings feelings of totality and integration beyond the problems of the moment. When we look at a beautiful painting, or become absorbed in painting ourselves, when we are executing an intricate athletic or dance movement, we become so totally involved in the perception that words, social meaning, and social values become nonexistent and unimportant. It is a feeling of aliveness and well-being. Most importantly, for cognitive organization, we experience a thought process which deals primarily with total impression, space, and images of the moment. The crucial concept which is missing is that of time. Without time we are lost in present experience, in reflection as if it were occurring now, and without any evaluation of right or wrong, good or bad. What is presently occurring in our perception is real at the intrapsychic level, and one of the highest forms of imagery production. We are visualizing, smelling, tasting, and experiencing without regard for time or logic.

For the classroom teacher it is important to recognize that this total awareness and involvement in space and imagery is without regard to logic, order, and sequence for these are all temporal or socialized forms of cognition. Most people can experience this mode of thought without difficulty and return, at any moment, to the more integrated naturalistic and social thought structure of consonant interhemispheric consciousness, or to a purely socialized consciousness. The Alpha child may have trouble returning to so-called "reality" of socialized or interhemispheric modes. He may have trouble returning to normalized consciousness because of poor language and socialized capacity, or he may be reluctant to do so, due to a need to escape responsibility or the joy of being in a fantasy world. But naturalized consciousness is not an unusual or alien means of perception; rather, it is an important part of each individual's total capacity to understand and interpret information from the world about him. Since the naturalistic mode involves much of the basic and earliest form of learning, it is a fundamental aspect of all thought. Socialized thinking is learned through the culture and gives rise to the order and structure which is nonexistent in the usual sense in naturalized thought.

Socialized Cognitive Function

Giving "meaning" to some perception or thought usually implies some sort of evaluation of the information. Beyond the simplest form of personal evaluation such as recognition of and seeking of pleasure, satisfaction of physiological needs, or a general feeling of good health, evaluation usually implies some sort of culturally learned concept. Evaluation serves to structure behavior toward some socially desired act or response. Cognition which involves ordering, serialization or sequence, spatial orientation within predetermined directional preferences, or giving a response or an act of social value are all socialized forms of thought. These are usually built upon the basic physiological needs but involve tendencies toward satisfaction of ego enhancement and social worth in addition to the physiological needs. For example, the young infant and child may want to play with a restricted object, move about in restricted areas, or act out his frustrations in aggressive ways which, to his naturalized and undeveloped thought process, fit the situation and his needs. In order to learn appropriate and secure ways to obtain satisfaction for needs, he must learn language and signal systems which place restrictions upon his impulsive and naturalistic behaviors. He has to learn many abstract and social concepts in order to "understand" appropriate ways to behave or "restrict" his own behavior. This we usually refer to as the socialization process and the development of independence. This growth involves a great variety of complex socialized behaviors. These behaviors and information related to them are defined here as socialized cognitive processes and, as has been stated, are functions primarily of left hemispheric development. This development, however, proceeds upon the basic structure of naturalized and sensory-oriented experience defined in the naturalized cognitive growth. Initial learning and awareness are natural and do not involve social thought or cognitions.

Socialization, relative to cognitive processing, is most dependent upon the element of time as opposed to naturalized thought which is built upon space and sensory information. Both forms of thought involve elements of time and space, but the major form of cognition in each hemisphere deals with the integration of either time or space processes. This is why the integration of the two forms of thought is so significant to the totally functioning of being.

The Naturalistic Foundation of Social Mindedness

For the first few months of the infant's life he is captured in timeless space. His only recognition of reality is the spatial world he views about him. During these months the foundation for understanding space begins through vision and body movement. Language and time are still unknown realities which lie in the incomprehensible future. The infant becomes aware of his muscular system and senses the information constantly being fed into his naturalized mode of information processing. He has little time to be concerned with the why or the when of his being. He slowly feels the sensory messages coming from his body and eventually learns to respond and to control first his head and neck and then later his limbs until finally he begins to make purposeful movements which turn and twist his body into better positions for learning more about his environment. To be sure, his socialized mind is already awakening and beginning to listen to speech sounds, and there is an emerging union between what he feels, sees, and hears. But his first task is that of conquering the space about him through ever more sophisticated control and awareness of his own body.

This earliest and most basic level of information processing is the first neurological system to become capable of organized awareness. It will remain the most fundamental and secure aspect of the child's being for the remainder of his life, even when socialized thought eventually gains mastery of the entire system.

By the time the child is a few weeks old another significant sensory process will have begun, emotional attachment. This process, first built upon the tactile and kinesthetic security of a mother's warmth and fondling, eventually develops into an internal recognition of security and of attachment to a human being, and the child begins to process information which will eventuate in the close relationship between the natural mind and emotions. Perhaps no other learning or development will be more significant to the child than this early association of warmth and security founded in the kinesthetic and tactile system. It will provide, for the child, a life-long chain of non-verbal and naturalistic behaviors which will require that he touch others for assurance of love, security, and relationships. It is here that the strongest neurological bonds are formed between emotion and cognitive structure. This is why all relationships, verbal and rational though they may be, must in their culmination eventuate in physical interaction to obtain the fullest recognition of love.

By the age of five years the child, through naturalized cognition, has established a complex system of spatial awareness which involves integration of movement through space. Space becomes a part of the internal being. The child moves an arm, a leg, or all of his limbs in coordination to execute complex movement through space. The child recognizes space, relative to himself, as existing above, behind, under, over, to each side, and at all points in between. The symphony of coordination required to move in predetermined ways in space provides the child with the mental structure to organize or to recognize differences in the sides of his body, of the location of sounds in relation to various spatial points about him, and to locate items relative to their spatial relationships to his body. As he conquers space and organizes it around his own body, his naturalized mind becomes a complex system of mathematical relationships. A movement of the arm can be a full swing to the right or left, from the side to full extension above the head, or in either direction at once. He learns to predict how to move in calibrated ways for partial movements to the left or right, up or down, forward or backward, and all of the diagonal possibilities of points in between. He learns to extend his arm half way, all the way, or to points in between in order to move, to grasp, to lift, or hit, or deflect. By the time a child is five years of age, he senses more mathematical calibrations and formulas for space and movement than he will learn to identify through symbolic mathematics during the remainder of his life. It will remain for his socialized cognitive structure to attempt to apply labels and symbols to such complex spatial capabilities.

Time and Temporal Organization

Before us is a child who extends his hand outward and moves it across a horizontal plane in front of his eyes. As his hand moves across the horizontal and vertical plane, time is created as the socialized left hemisphere begins its nearly mystical growth in learning the passing of time. In that moment our child becomes distinctly human and elevates himself forever above the capacities of lower animals.

With space conquered the child can now begin to conceptualize division of space and designate certain areas of space to symbolize before and after, left to right, and specialized segmenting of space to imply equal units. The mother, pleading with the child to take his first independent step, says "come here." With her arms outstretched toward him he receives both the verbal and spatial message to move toward her. In this way and thousands of others he begins to give space and directions verbal meaning, a symbolic representation of space. The child takes his first step toward her and with her social praise he begins to integrate space and time. He learns verbal meaning for his spatial world.

Throughout the first five years the child slowly develops his movement and spatial awareness and integrates language into the total conception of integration of naturalized and socialized thought. The simple word "were" is understood spatially, as well as temporally, to mean the past or what was before. For most children, this spatial and temporal concept is represented by space to the left on a time line. If it is Friday, then Monday has passed to the left, just as April is to the left of June and August to the right of June. "Now" becomes this minute; "later," the one directly ahead. One hour ago becomes some spatial distance to the left and one hour from now becomes a spatial distance to the right. Numbers proceed from left to right, and words provide, finally, a symbolic representation of time. Five feet tall becomes higher or further up the numerical scale than four feet. Three feet is shorter, further down than five feet. Distance becomes a verbal concept representing a point somewhere to the left or right, in front or behind, a continuum of points or a horizontal line, or any number of other possibilities in which space can be designated as a specific motor and kinesthetic correlate.

Time and Language

Language is the mechanism of time. Time becomes a designated movement or division of space into units. The hands of a clock, interestingly enough, move from left to right in a clockwise motion. The digital clock consists of passing numbers which move forward indicating a movement of time. Spelling and reading consist of interpreting phonetic sounds in a sequential movement from left to right. In this way both numbers and words, symbolic representations of space, conceptualize a movement from left to right or the passing of time.

Language, utilizing spatial constructs first learned in the natural mind, becomes a representation of reality and allows us to reflect upon ourselves in the passing moment and to predict either our own behavior or that of others in the future. In this way we can "conceptualize" ourselves and compare ourselves to others in a variety of ways. This ability allows us to evaluate, to measure, to compare, and to estimate or predict. Finally, language becomes the servant of memory, in that information stored within the hemispheres can be located in past time and recalled for present use.

Memory is very dependent upon spatial organization just as is time. The socialized mind, through its development upon the spatial learning of the natural mind, is able to structure complex abstractions and classifications which would be difficult without the cooperation of both the natural and socialized mind structures. This is why integration of the two forms of thought is so important not only to learning but to the development of self-concept and awareness.

Behavior and Time

When the child develops adequate language to reflect upon himself and others, he begins the true socialized stage of development where he begins to evaluate his behavior in reference to others. In this way he can learn appropriate behavior to gain approval, recognition, and rewards. The severely retarded child, the disturbed child, or the brain-damaged child may have trouble with social behavior and make modifications which will allow them to avoid negative consequences. Impulsive behavior is often behavior which results from simply acting out in ways which are not mediated by the use of language and memory. This child is able to recognize desired goals, but he is unable to conceptualize time and space relationships making it difficult or impossible to predict future consequences based on past experience. He understands no cause-and-effect relationship. The difficulty began with inadequate spatial, naturalized learning and eventuated in poor language and time organization.

Language as a Mediator in Behavior

If a child spatially conceptualizes an apple and wants someone to give him one, he must describe this conceptualization in abstractions called words and understand the future consequences of asking for an apple. In this example the child's physiological system communicates to the natural mind an object which will satisfy a basic need of hunger. The socialized mind then translates this message into language and time along with the appropriate behaviors which will eventuate in satisfying the need. This is an example of how socialization allows for obtaining need satisfaction through integration of interhemispheric cooperation and thoughts. It can be said that language is the mediator of behavior. Without language or organized thought relative to time and space, the child would have to search about for an apple until he found one. Since the apple may not be in the immediate space, then he must resort to the use of language to describe what he wants to the appropriate adults who he *expects* will be able to locate the desired object.

Mediation is that process whereby the two hemispheres can be utilized to conceptualize and organize behavior in ways which will gain needed behavior outcomes. Mediation is the process of modifying behavior toward desired goals. Without language the child would be unable to "logically" manipulate his environment, and he would be unable to effectively evaluate the behavior of others.

Values define how behavior will be structured to reach goals. The child learns the "language" values of behavior through social modeling and information stored in the socialized mind. Values would be most difficult to learn without abstraction provided through language, for values not only describe the "why" but also the "how" of mediated behavior. The child begins to learn social values even prior to the development of formal language. When the child begins to cross a street or touch a hot object, the parent responds with facial expressions and movements which the child is able to understand nonverbally as meaning "that is not a good thing to do." This naturalized communication is nonverbal and makes up a vast store of behavior knowledge long before the child learns the language concepts associated with right or wrong. As language is learned, the child learns words for the already existent nonverbal mediators. Words such as "no," "don't," "bad," and "stop" are initially learned in very direct relationships to already existent nonverbal knowledge. As language and time constructs are developed, the child becomes more sophisticated in his understanding of values.

The most powerful initial nonverbal value learnings are those attached to the withdrawal of love or affection. These values eventually become language constructs associated with self-concept. Not only are behaviors identified as bad and as having negative consequences, but the child learns that negative behavior also suggests that the "self" is bad as well as the behavior. The child, in his increasing need to gain personal acceptance and praise, learns how to behave in order to obtain love and affection. One acts like a "good" boy or girl. Acting like a "good" boy or girl requires the ability to remember past behavior and to predict future behavior relative to desired consequences. Social values become attached to and are built on spatial or naturalized concepts of space along with socialized constructs of time.

Concepts of time are quite complex and involve ever more sophisticated relationships between time and space as the child grows. But it is unlikely that any child can learn abstraction in language without adequate perceptual and motoric experience upon which such learning can be developed. This is why a child may learn the phonetic and perceptual correlates of many words but not be able to "comprehend" what the words or sentences mean. If the child has no concrete experience upon which to base his phonetic learning, then learning to read is a meaningless task.

The teacher and parent may now begin to understand why both motoric experience and language experience are so critical, not only to effective communication but also to the development of values and personality.

Integration Functions

When the child reaches the age of approximately six years, extensive "interhemispheric" growth begins which gives rise to more complex processes in both hemispheres. Obviously, the age of six years does not mark the end of any specific developmental process or the beginning of another. All children vary greatly in the rate and quality of their cognitive growth. Nevertheless, at approximately the age of six years most children are experiencing a significant growth in neurological integrative capacity. This involves the coming together, the melding, the integration of many forms of perceptual and cognitive functions which have been developing more or less independently. As the child is able to comprehend more and more abstract and remote relationships he integrates information from both the natural and socialized thought process into summated insights. Summation can be considered that process which requires both hemispheres in order to comprehend the totality of an event or idea. The integration of naturalized and socialized thought processes results in the following examples of behavior.

RECOGNITION OF THE RELATIONSHIPS OF TIME AND SPACE. The child is able to divide space conceptually into units which relate to left and right and up and down. While other directional coordinates are also learned these two provide a significant mental function. They allow the child to relate present events to those in the past and to possible consequences in the future. This gives a flexible and developmental capacity to thought. The child can perceive how his present behavior is similar to past behavior and on that comparison he can predict and alter his behavior in inventive ways.

SOCIAL VALUES ARE ENHANCED FOR NOW THE CHILD CAN COMPREHEND THE MEANING OF PRESENT AND FUTURE BEHAVIOR BASED UPON THE FAMILIARITY OR PRESENT FACTORS TO THOSE OF THE PAST. He can begin to formulate "reasons" for behaving in a certain manner in the present situation. He is able to apply values he has learned in new situations and generalize them to situations which "might" occur.

THE CHILD IS ABLE TO MENTALLY REPRODUCE AND RECALL PAST EXPERIENCE THROUGH IMAGERY AND MANIPULATE THESE EXPERIENCES BY IMAGINING NEW EXPERIENCES. This abstraction of memory experiences allows the child to mentally manipulate images of more than one object or event to observe and discriminate similarities and differences between objects and events. This increases his ability to classify and to categorize vast amounts of information so that abstract language labels can be used for representing the experiences with the events and objects. He is able to see more and more remote associations in behavior and events.

THE CHILD IS ABLE TO VISUALIZE COMPLEX STRUCTURES, MAKE CHANGES IN THEIR PROPOSED FORM, AND CREATE THE ACTUAL MODEL WITHOUT PRIOR PRACTICE. This form of thought relates also to mental practice in body movements. The child can now talk abstractly about "things" experiences, and possible experiences and consequences in the future. This allows him to consider, through language imagery, such things as color, shape, size, texture, and behavior in the abstract. He can "picture" in his mind possible things he would like to build or do and construct them in the abstract. He can even make changes in his ideas until he finally actually builds or acts out his premeditated and designed action. This sort of function is also used in mentally practicing movements such as in sports.

THE CHILD CAN NOW MODEL AND DEVELOP LONG-TERM PATTERNS OF BEHAVIOR TO REACH DESIRED PERSONAL GOALS AND STATUS. The boy may want to be a fireman such as on the television show "Emergency." The girl may want to be the first airline pilot. Each of these goals may provide a long term model for the child causing him to structure his behavior through successive approximations in order to become the desired individual. The child adopts some sort of concrete social value model and then internally imagines behaviors and activities which will take him or her toward this goal over a long period of time. While these goals may be the immature dreams of a child initially, such mental practice using language, social models, and spatial imagery can provide a stream of consciousness which will guide the child's behavior for some time. This sort of practice lays the basis for personal discipline which will later be used to reach real personal occupational goals.

The foregoing capacities are only examples of the many processes which are summated through interhemispheric functions and are capacities dependent upon the child's ability to utilize both naturalized and socialized thought in one integrated process. Such a capability gives the child higher thought process skills and raises him beyond the elementary levels of lateralized or independent thought processes of either thought form alone. The training of formalized education provides the child with experience and practice in developing integrated thought capacity. School is mental practice.

Except for some perceptual processes, all activity in one hemisphere is monitored by the other hemisphere through neurological connective tissue between the two hemispheres. It is this connection which allows for communication of information between the two hemispheres. Since each hemisphere is the neurological opposite or mirror image of the other, much information is learned in a spatially reverse way, but this is not a problem since the dominant hemisphere is the seat of its own particular information, and when it mediates or processes information its own spatial orientation allows utilization of the information effectively.

The interconnectedness of the two hemispheres allows for integration of information and subsequent capacity to utilize information in a number of ways which would not be possible without this cooperation and communication. Further, there are many higher mental processes which would not be possible if such a connection were not present. A particular event or thought can be fixed in memory by a combination of several cognitive points involving both hemispheres. For example, a simple notion about the behavior of dogs can be expanded into a complex concept through the use of both hemispheres. The natural mind will observe the behavior of various dogs, and the child can develop several potential responses to dogs. He will learn about the different colors, sizes, hair textures, and behavior of dogs solely through naturalized and sensory perception. He can learn how to manage, train, and care for dogs through this thought mode alone. But with the addition of language, he can use words to order and classify all of their characteristics. The left hemisphere and language allows the child to predict and manipulate potential behaviors of dogs in new ways. He can learn about dogs from around the world, about the history of a particular breed, about the anatomy and health care of dogs, and classify large amounts of information quickly without the actual experience with each element. This blending of both naturalized experience and socialized language allows the child to develop many different perceptions and abstract neurological points of reference throughout both the right and left hemisphere. This interhemispheric activity provides a complex number of neurological points of reference about a single topic. This summated learning and experience is easily retained, because it has so many points of interconnectedness in rather remote areas of the two hemispheres. This is what may be called "long term" or permanent memory. This information is permanent in that it has a physical locus within the brain. There are actual naturalized and socialized brain tissue clusters which retain and hold this information. The more points of reference and the more remote their location, the more likely the child will retain and recall much information about dogs. When the child experiences, reads, or hears a new bit of information about dogs, he can refer to the many points of reference within the two systems and see if it "makes sense." If it does appear logical, agrees with enough known information, then it is easily added to the present structure of information and quickly becomes permanent learning. The phrase "making sense" is much more descriptive than most of us would imagine. It most likely evolved out of the experience of individuals who found that new information sometimes could not be correlated with "sense" information.

The more unique new information is, relative to our past experience, the more likely we will have to explore it first through basic sensory information, rather than through language structure. This correlates well with the nature of how the cerebral system initially developed. The spatial-perceptual system, the naturalized mind, was the earliest and most basic system of organization which the child learned. In situations where a totally new experience occurs, the child tends to revert back to this initial and, therefore, most comfortable level of learning. This is much like our experience with an unfamiliar object. First we touch, taste, smell, feel texture, and manipulate an object in order to later classify it and relate it to our more abstract language system. The more diverse and extensive our learning becomes, the less frequently we have to refer back to this level of behavior. The game of "Twenty Questions" is a good example. By knowing many linguistic classifications and verbal methods of eliminating alternates, we can, through verbal question, narrow potential objects and thoughts to the needed response. The less experience and language development we accumulate, 'the less able we are to succeed in such a game. Conversely, the more remote and unfamiliar the desired response, the more basic our questions must become in order to discover the desired response. In this way we can see how naturalized experience leads to socialized abstraction, a relationship having important implications in the teaching of children.

This process of ever-increasing integration and summation of information leads to higher and higher thought processes. After such processes have reached a complex level, even deterioration or damage to the system will not totally destroy the capacity of the system. Because any single memory trace is connected to so many remote points within the system, localized damage will not affect the entire memory capacity for any specific concept. Conversely, brain damage, cultural deprivation, poor learning initially, and a host of metabolic or functional disorders in the system during the early years can diminish the potential capacity of the system to develop such remote associations and summations. We may speculate, therefore, that minor genetic or cultural deficits early in life can have much more significance to the child's capacities than even significant damage or deterioration following adolescence and into adulthood. This is why early training and experience are so important as compared to later deprivation or impairment of the system. It is true that we do not merely teach or parent children, we actually provide their environment from the day they are born well into childhood. Their cognitive structure is not simply "there" nor does it simply "grow;" it is created through experience and opportunity. Such a weightly responsibility falls upon the schools and community, as well as on the parents. It is bad enough that we may prevent a child from learning to read; it is unthinkable that we may actually limit his capacity to "be." These following points will be used in the ensuing discussion to clarify factors in the home and learning environments of children which are important to providing positive and effective instruction.

1. The child first learns and develops awareness of his physical and emotional environment through naturalized or right hemispheric maturation.
2. Sensory-motor learning, while an interhemispheric activity, is predominantly a naturalized function and is lateralized in the right hemisphere.
3. Naturalized perception involves an understanding and synthesis of sensory information concerning vision, nonlanguage sounds, smell, taste, tactile and kinesthetic data.
4. Initial self awareness, or consciousness, develops as a consequence of naturalized perceptual processes.
5. Naturalized thought processes of perception, synthesis, memory, and analysis relate directly to personal needs without the utilization of social values and language.
6. Naturalized thought provides the spatial organization upon which language can be utilized to formulate concepts of time, serialization, specific spatial and directional organization, and predictability of behavior and external events.
7. Language, primarily integrated with socialized awareness in the left hemisphere, develops as a secondary maturation process, built upon and consonant with naturalized maturation.
8. Physical self-awareness is extended abstractly through the use of language symbols which represent the self and which is defined here as "socialized consciousness." An individual modulates personal consciousness between socialized and naturalized awareness into an internal unity.
9. While an individual may have a specific motoric dominance, he also develops a generalized cerebral dominance which may or may not be in the same hemisphere as motor dominance.
10. Motor dominance includes not only body locomotion preferences in handedness and footedness, but also in visual dominance.
11. Body awareness and concept along with the establishment

of motoric dominance play a major role in eventual establishment of spatial-temporal organization.

12. Cerebral dominance and interhemispheric integration provides personality and social behavioral preferences beyond motoric dominance which can affect learning.

13. Socialized individuals may be called "left minded" while naturalized individuals are referred to as "right minded." These terms designate tendencies toward preference in one consciousness mode or the other.

14. Individuals who develop the usual socialized dominance in hemispheric structure are able to organize their behavior effectively in both learning and social value environments.

15. Individuals who develop an atypical naturalized hemispheric dominance may have difficulty in understanding or adjusting to social value expectations and the typically "right-handed" structure of education.

16. Instructional programs must be designed to provide not only specialized remedial assistance for naturalized individuals, but special aspects of the educational program should be designed so that naturalized individuals can learn through their own special mode of organization.

17. School curricula should be designed so that both naturalized and socialized neurological functions are stimulated in all children for maximum development of both capacities.

18. The major aim of education should be to stimulate integration of right mindedness and left mindedness in all children toward a high level of neurological development and integration.

19. Synthesis of logical and socially oriented left mindedness with the creative and natural right mindedness of each individual provides the greatest possible personal potential in human awareness.

20. Left mindedness represents primarily Western culture, social, and religious philosophy while right mindedness represents primarily Eastern culture and thought. One is logical and orderly with the other being holistic and mystical.

REFERENCE

1. Bloom, B. et al.: *Taxonomy of Educational Objectives: The Classification of Educational Goals, Handbook II, Affective Domain.* New York, McKay, 1956.

Chapter 5

PERSONALITY DEVELOPMENT

Tomorrow will demand much of its children, for they must become total beings capable of creative and flexible thought tempered with reason and logic. There will always be the dreamers with high levels of naturalized capacities and intuition, just as there must always be the scientists and reasonable thinkers who meet the practical needs of the culture. Within the culture there will be populations of individuals who cannot afford the luxury of being solely creative or strictly technological, for most of the population will have to be capable of maintaining society and setting about the task of everyday living. While some individuals will be the creative or technological thinkers who provide the means of societal adaptive potential, the usual individual will need to be much more capable of both creative and technological behaviors than is the case today. Much will be demanded of tomorrow's children. The essential key to man's survival capacities has always been his ability to adapt. The success of each individual is dependent upon his ability to adapt not only to the pace and complexity of the society but to his own being through various stages of his life. This adaptation is possible through the complex and ever-evolving factor of cognitive synthesis.

Cognitive Synthesis and Personality

Cognitive synthesis is not an easy concept to grasp, and yet for teachers it is a most important element which affects higher learning. To understand cognitive synthesis and to provide the educational environment within which it can be developed one must reach far beyond the more typical concerns of learning to read, to write, or to remember the dates of important historical events. Subject matter is the material upon which effective cognitive synthesis is built. Cognitive synthesis is the true goal of learning. Children may be taught facts and calculations, but they must learn to "think" and to find some meaning to their being. It is one thing to provide guidance to children so that they may learn the tools of the culture in the form of language and values; it is far more difficult to provide the environment within which they can utilize those tools in discovering meaning and reason for their behavior. The latter is what makes education the most important endeavor in the culture, and it is the goal which education appears to find the most difficult to achieve. Much has been said here about naturalized and socialized growth relative to mental processes. The mental processes involved in naturalized thought give the child the ability to understand his sensory world, to organize and understand spatial information, and to develop intuition and insight through a "gestalt" of nonverbal information. The mental processes of socialized thought provide the child with the facility to order, to symbolize, to organize, and to evaluate information. These two forms of thought can be incorporated and synthesized to achieve a higher level of awareness and personality than can be achieved through either process alone. The child who learns predominantly naturalistic thought processes to the detriment of the socialized capacities will develop distinctive personality and perceptual characteristics, just as the converse will be true of the highly socialized thinker. Cognitive synthesis is the theoretical integration of competent and fully developed capacities in both forms of thought into the highest level of human behavior. When specific processes within one form of thought become dominant, the individual is less able to develop his fullest capacities. Education can be and is the most formidable intervention in the prevention of poorly developed capacities in one form of thought over the other.

The Dependence of Cognitive Synthesis Upon Learning

We have reviewed, in previous chapters, how the child *learns* first in the naturalistic mode of thought and perception. How well the child initially learns depends upon the nature of his environment and the basic integrities of his genetic endowment. Certainly, the child who has genetic defects, prenatal neurological insults, or nutritional deficiencies will come into the world with less potental to learn in either the naturalistic or socialized neurostructures. Such deficits will affect the child's learning potential. But given at least an even chance at birth most children will learn effectively if the environment provides adequate nurturance and opportunity. To the degree that specific deficits are existent in naturalistic processes, subsequent effects will be noted in both eventual naturalized thinking and socialized capacities. Both genetic and environmental factors can act to lower eventual integration of total potentials within the two thought modes. Since it is not our concern here to discuss genetic or prenatal defects, our assumption will be that whatever learning the child achieves is basically dependent upon opportunity and environment.

The early learning of the child appears to gain some permanence relative to adult potential. Early childhood learning provides an initial base of information for the child, and it structures the brain in personal ways of responding to the environment. These early learned structures affect a "mind set," so to speak, upon which all subsequent learning will be perceived and developed. The brain becomes "conditioned" to perceive environmental information relative to early learned factors. This is as true with specific perceptual sets as it is with social learning. The earlier specific learning occurs, the more permanent and difficult to change it becomes. Such learning can even affect an individual's adult responses. If a child is treated cruelly during his first two years, his brain structure develops specific ways of responding to other individuals which are difficult to change even though the individual later learns new information. Such cruelty early in life may set a particular mode of response to others which is cautious and prevents effective formation of interpersonal relationships. The child may require many years of successful peer and adult interactions before the early learning is finally overcome. Even though the individual eventually learns to love, to show warmth, and to trust others, in situations where there is a high degree of threat or confrontation he may regress to his early response modes. It is doubtful that we erase completely those responses which we learned early in life.

When the young child is initially learning naturalistic and socialized thought processes, much of the brain in unstructured, poorly organized, and open to rapid and extensive growth. This period of high receptivity is thought to occur particularly between birth and the end of the eighth year. As a result, the child has developed an extensive "mind set" and permanent structure of behavioral responses by the time he enters school. If the child's early environment has prepared him adequately, then he is "ready" to learn formal information. However, if the child has developed poor naturalized and socialized information, the beginning of formal education may be difficult. This is why so many children require additional time, at the outset of formal education, to become appropriately receptive and able to learn formal information.

There is little doubt that the period from preschool and kindergarten throughout the first two grades are the most significant years of formal education for all children. Interestingly enough, it has only been in recent years that educators and parents have come to accept early childhood education as important. The child who has poor motoric experiences often comes to kindergarten unable to learn the fine motor, perceptual, and language skills necessary for cutting, coloring, listening, and communicating. This child has not developed adequate body concept, lateral control of the body, balance, and effective movement in gross motor function. Such deficits illustrate a poor development of naturalized abilities and skills. The child's self-concept of his physical behavior will be poor, just as later language and socialized concept may also suffer. The child's personality and behavioral traits will reflect this poor motoric and language development. Since learning is naturalized and socialized function have been impaired, the child's ability to integrate these two areas of development will also be impaired.

Some children develop adequate perceptual-motor function but have a poor early language environment. The parents talk little with the child and most family interaction involves only primitive language which is used to express motoric or aggressive behavior. Without adequate language, the child will tend to overdevelop and utilize naturalistic behavioral styles. Certainly, the general personality of such a child can become one of acting out behavior, "fight or flight" responses, and a tendency to avoid formal learning.

Many children today receive poor early motoric and perceptual stimulation and a high level of language indoctrination. These children often develop highly sophisticated verbal skills but are poorly adapted in motoric and naturalistic skills. Such children can become quite manipulative of adults and use verbal skills to avoid responsibility or adhering to adult direction. Their personalities are often ego-centered and self-indulgent because they have learned early how to manipulate others to serve their needs.

There is little doubt that the early learning of the child not only can shape personality but lay the basis for it. But, just as learning can cause maladaptive behavior, so can learning in an effective school or home environment alter such behavior. This is the task of education, not so much to merely teach the child, but to assure that he develops adequate naturalized and socialized capacities toward eventual integration and cognitive synthesis at the highest possible level. Early learning provides the "mind set" for future adaptive abilities. It is this mind structure and synthesis which is even more critical to the child than simply learning the tools of academic activities. Recognizing the importance of early learning, educators must begin to differentiate the school curriculum toward both naturalized and socialized learning aside from content learning. We are not just teaching skills; we are teaching personality and synthesis capacity.

Traditional Concepts of Personality

Personality has often been thought of as a "thing," an entity within, or a synthesis of behavioral characteristics which are perceived by another individual. Personality, in more clinical terms, has usually been considered that central core of self-awareness and being which distinguishes one individual from another. Those interested in personality have previously focused study on the various aspects of personal perception and behavior. More recently, many of the traditional concepts of personality have come to be considered more and more from a "learning theory" viewpoint by many professionals in psychology. The learning theory viewpoint does not see the individual or personality as something controlled by the mercy of some sort of hidden intrapsychic factors. Rather the personality is seen as something that is learned and can be altered to some degree through additional information. For parents and teachers, the learning theory approach is perhaps the most practical with children.

Many psychologists have assumed that one of the major conflicts for the young child in development of a healthy personality is the conflict between the basic egocentric or self-centered tendency to serve one's own needs and the demands of the society requiring that each individual "modulate" his behavior relative to social rules and values. How well the child learns to modulate his needs within the value structure of the culture determines how "adjusted" his personality becomes. This concept of personality development is one of the great human dramas and involves the notion that all individuals are motivated toward serving their basic needs or, as it was once called, drive system. It is fairly easy for us to understand that the young infant is somewhat "ego-centered" and seeks to obtain food, comfort, nurturance, and security. These are obvious and basic needs of all human beings. While the infant may learn quickly that mother will come when summoned by an instant cry, he also soon learns that this is not always the case. Socialization begins early as the mother attempts to get the child on a regular sleep and feeding cycle. The infant must learn to adhere to such a schedule and, with physiological maturation, he finds it possible to do so. But in the process the child is learning to "modulate" his behavior or to accept certain limits on his own egocentric needs. As the young child matures, he learns social values such as conforming to group membership rules where he must wait in line, share attention of adults with other peers, and behave in such ways as to obtain recognition, social praise, and group esteem. Eventually, the child has a growing social need to be accepted and to increase his own self-esteem and personal value. Social needs become nearly as important as if not more important than, the basic physiological needs.

Learning theory would suggest that elements of personality development are learned by both normal development and maturation of the nervous system and the interaction of this maturation with the cultural environment. How well the child learns to modulate and control his behavior determines how well he will be able to control basic drive impulses in socially acceptable ways.

One of the problems for parents and teachers in understanding personality development has been the difficulty with many of the technical concepts and with the problem of relating such concepts to the child's behavior in the classroom. Parents today have become quite sophisticated in their knowledge of possible phobias and traumas which may be created over potty training or bouts at the dinner table as the child is exposed to initial socialization expectations. Modern child-rearing practices tend to emphasize the concept of democratic and logical approaches to child management, and punishment has become an unacceptable means to control or socialize the behavior of the child in many homes. Children are encouraged to explore and question values as a means of assisting them in understanding the logic of certain behavioral expectations. While there is little doubt that punishment is the least effective way to develop open and healthy personalities, many democratic and modern child-rearing practices have been used with too little understanding by parents and teachers. Certainly, we are not planning to engage in a discussion of child-rearing practices here, but parents and teachers may benefit from a different viewpoint concerning personality development and the management of behavior in children.

Differential Neuro-Learned Personality Factors

An essential aspect of early childhood development is the

emergence of self-awareness. This awareness may be called "ego-consciousness" and is first established upon sensory-motor development throughout the first year of life. At birth the infant has no information upon which to evaluate or measure himself as a distinct and separate being. He simply responds to his physiological needs which create stress within the physical system, resulting in cries of displeasure. These cries are responded to by nursing, holding and fondling, and care by the mother. At this point the infant knows little of who is feeding or fondling him, but each day the infant accumulates information concerning his biological system and the responses of those about him. Through the first year the infant develops increasing personal awareness and differentiation not only of his own physical self but of separate entities about him. This learning is based primarily upon sensory feedback, though he is also learning some elements of language sounds. At this early stage the infant responds to touch, temperature, taste, smell, and kinesthetic movement within his system and those about him. The initial formation of "ego-awareness" is growing each day, and this awareness is centered in naturalized or right hemispheric information. Because this early development is so dependent upon sensory information synthesized in the right hemisphere, the child's earliest emotional feelings are learned in relation to primary sensory information. This early bond between primitive emotions and sensory-based naturalized awareness, forms a lasting and powerful learning relationship which will affect the child throughout his life. As the child takes his first steps, says his first word, and suffers his first reprimand for wandering too far from mother, he is constantly learning ego identity or self-awareness. This early nonverbal learning and structuring of personality includes feelings of positive and negative self-awareness. The child who receives much encouragement from his parents continues to explore with feelings of security and wonder. But the child who is not encouraged, who meets with constant frustration from adults about him, or who finds little security in his world will develop self-doubt and poor self-awareness. This fundamental basis for personality is the earliest and most permanent learning. All later learning will to some degree meet with the structure of this earliest self-awareness and the positive or negative quality of the child's inner feelings.

The ego identity of the naturalized self is very important as a basis for later development of successful socialized learning. It is essential to remember that the naturalized information is now endowed with the logical evaluation characteristics of the socialized self. The child develops nonverbal and naturalized self-awareness during those first years, but he does not evaluate its relative goodness or badness. The early self-consciousness does not have the capacity to reflect or to predict, and, therefore, much of this awareness is an ego-centered and selfish style of being. If language and socialized awareness evolves in an atmosphere of security and love, then the child "accepts" the limitations of social learning upon his naturalized self as a consequence of trust and love which he has "learned" to expect and desire. Conversely, if this early stage of ego development is marked by rejection, anxiety, conflict, or deprivation, the child may continue his selfish and naturalistic behaviors as a means of personal survival. This negative self-awareness prevents acceptance or the development of trust upon which eventual socialization will depend. It may be that eventual development of language and social awareness will simply provide an extension of skills in avoidance of relationships, in serving (through manipulation) one's own selfish needs, and in a lack of cooperative skills so needed in the formal learning program. Such difficulties will prevent the effective interfunction of neurological development between naturalized and socialized thought. Such a child may remain an isolated and distrustful individual who has a drastic reduction in cognitive synthesis capacity, in that the basic naturalized self utilizes language to serve its selfish ends rather than developing the full capacities of the socialized potential for integration. To alter such a state of awareness takes many years in an effective and nurturing environment.

This concept of personality formation and development is based upon learning experience and the child's adaptive responses to such learning. The child proceeds, through a natural sequence of learning, from merely responding undifferentially to external and internal sensory information to an early ego structure as a result of learning perceptual information about his environment and internal differentiation of neurological mechanisms. This first stage of personality development allows the emergence of naturalized self-awareness through sensory and primary emotional attachment. This stage provides for the first level of ego-awareness, that state of internal differentiation of self from the environment. At this level the child is already experiencing language and processing basic associations between behavior feelings, sensory information, and linguistic structure. During the latter part of the first year, language appears as "ma-ma," and the socialized structure truly begins.

At this earliest level of ego-awareness, the child is self-centered, and his world evolves around him for he does not yet know of the complex nature of the world outside his own view and experience. However, he already has feelings of inner centralness which are nonverbal and rooted in his own sensory awareness of himself as a being separate from those about him. For the next two years he will continue to attempt to control his environment through crying, babbling, and simple words or phrases. His basic emotions will change from simple feelings of frustration and primitive rage in response to not receiving need gratification, to feelings of positive self-awareness including basic pleasure, surprise and joy, primary anger over unexpected intrusions on his behavior, and laughter when feelings of happiness pervade his sensory world.

During the second to fourth years, the child will change rapidly into a social being as he learns to modulate his behavior in response to the behavior of others about him. His being is such that a laugh is but a step away from a tear; his is a world of quickly changing emotion and uncontrolled reaction. It is the March of the child's life. He attempts to retain his direction and determination, to explore whatever pleases him and to run unhindered through his world. But he is already learning of the pleasures of being loved, gaining verbal praises and recognition, and being accepted by others. He is extending his ego-awareness through the natural sequence of ever-expanding capacity and knowledge, to include linguistic impressions and evaluations of both himself and others. He finds joy in being able to name and tell of things, to find out the nature of objects and people about him, to find his place within the extending perceptual environment in which he finds himself. He is at once clinging to egocentric desires and reaching out for greater status among those about him. The naturalized self is giving way to the structure and order of socialized thinking.

In this second stage of personality development, the emergence of the socialized self, the child is now building upon his original naturalized behavioral structure. This building is not so much a "putting away" of the naturalized self as it is a further differentiation of the natural self. The success of these phases of self and ego-awareness will be determined by how the child develops socialized self-awareness or ego structure. If there are inaccuracies in the basic naturalized self-awareness, these can be changed to some degree by effective socialization, but it is doubtful that the effects of naturalized foundations in ego structure will ever be completely altered. It is a matter of effective socialized differentiation of what is already there and not the development of some sort of "new" ego structure which negates or completely changes the basic and naturalized ego. An understanding of this factor is very important in meeting the growing ego needs of the child as he enters school and proceeds into adolescence.

The development of the neurological structure in the right hemisphere proceeds first during the initial stages of development. While many aspects of left hemispheric development are utilized during this initial stage, it is hypothesized that the essential control of the organism is through the right hemisphere. The basic ego definition, then, is that self of early experiences and information which the child learned during the first year or so of life. During the second phase, language and social behavior are developed as a further sophistication and differentiation of that natural self. To this degree, the left hemisphere, the language center, is an outgrowth of the directions set by the naturalized ego structure. By the time a child is between two and three years of age, much of his general personality potential for the remainder of his life will have been organized. Socialization, if it is impressively successful, can alter to some degree the directions and characteristics of the ego structure of early life, but it will not change the most basic personal, mental sets neurologically structured during this early and most fundamental state of being. This is why the first two or three years of a child's life are perhaps the most significant. From the second to third years through the eighth, socialization and the development of a complex differential ego structure continues. After the age of eight years it becomes increasingly difficult to alter the child's ego structure, his complex personality matrix, or his behavioral tendency toward actualizing whatever he has come to be. The brain organization, ego structure, and permanent cement of life patterns will have been set.

The third stage is this final stage of personality and ego formation which lasts essentially from the fourth to eighth year. It is during this period that the left hemisphere or socialized ego structure is finally organized. In this stage the child learns and establishes personality factors based upon his experience with social values, the nature of social interaction and all of its ramifications, and the nature of the learning environment.

All of these factors are dependent upon several significant variables related to learning and neurological structuring of the central nervous system, particularly in the form of the left and right hemispheres. The development of a human being is *not* merely a work of creation based upon unknowledgeable love; the creation of a human being is a painful and tedious responsibility. The great artist gives birth to art not through blind love but through years of training and frustrations. Can the creation of a human being be any less of a challenge? Acceptance of parenthood is *not* something that should be the result of selfish love between two adults, *but* rather the careful consideration of the responsibility which creation brings. That we understand the nature of our inner selves and, therefore, the complexity of rearing a child is to experience it in full awareness rather than merely a passionate encounter.

Deviant Behavior Syndrome

Some children are defined as exhibiting a syndrome of *"primitive and unsocialized"* deviant behavior. These children often come from deprived socioeconomic groups and exhibit behavior which is aggressive, hostile, and devoid of the seemingly appropriate social values or socialized behaviors needed to adapt in the community or at school. Their behavior is primitive in that they respond to threat with flight or fight behaviors rather than using language to intervene in their responses. The ego structure of these children is characterized by impulsive and need gratification behaviors which usually make them poor students and unable to delay gratification. They often fail in school with particular difficulties in reading and language arts.

While the primitive-unsocialized child may be a child who has some sort of organic or neurological disorder, more often than not he exhibits behavior which results from a severe developmental and cultural deficit. Characteristics of this child are his impulsiveness, lack of control, negativeness, inability to delay gratification, and generally unsocialized personality structure. This child is fixated in the naturalistic realm of perception and consciousness. He is the naturalistic child unbounded and nurtured in an environment of hostility, punitiveness, and a lack of trust. How could this happen? In that the child has not developed adequate controls upon his behavior, it can be assumed that socialized development has not been adequately learned. He has matured within a naturalistic mode of thought without subsequent development of the socializing effect of language and values.

The primitive and unsocialized child is developmentally fixated at the naturalistic mode of functioning. Further, this level of mental operation has been conditioned in an environment of rejection and insecurity. Such a child does not learn a close attachment to his mother early in life and fails to gain the security and positive feedback needed to develop an accepting and trusting natural relationship. Instead, this child learns how to avoid, to escape, and to fight for his basic needs. This requires much energy, and the usual patterns of social information are not experienced or learned.

This child is operating much like a frightened animal who is unable to reason or to learn from new experiences. Even more important is the effect of such development on the early psycho-neuro-structure of the brain. The child is learning, but his learning is used for defensive and offensive behaviors as a means of personal survival. Cognitive structure which is developed for this purpose tends to lay the basis for mental sets which will later be unreceptive to change toward positive development without extensive and patient efforts from teachers and parents. This child is neurologically crippled just as if there had been actual neurological damage. Fortunately, the primitive-unsocialized child does offer a greater likelihood of responsiveness to effective learning environments than the child with brain damage.

The primitive child must be approached through both naturalized and socialized teaching techniques. This child must be identified early, in either preschool or kindergarten, if significant change is to be achieved. The teacher will have to hold and touch the child in accepting and nurturing ways to give the nonverbal assurance of security, for this is the consciousness mode in which the child is most likely to understand communication. Such a child will have to continually test the adult, for he already has a long history of learning which suggests that adults cannot be trusted regardless of how his natural tendencies and need for affection trigger a desire to give in. The teacher should be prepared to be pinched, kicked, hit, or even bitten depending on how he may be responding. The child will be torn between wanting to be loved and intense anxiety and fear when he finds himself letting down his defenses. But slowly, after first acceptance and then aggression, the child will eventually respond more and more to the positive and continually accepting approach of the adult. Setbacks will be inevitable but should not cause the teacher to give up or respond to aggression with aggression.

Once the child begins to place some trust in an adult, language must slowly be encouraged through talking to the child and encouraging him to talk, to learn values, and to seek ways of successfully behaving in order to gain the positive attention and friendship of his peers. All of this can take one, two, or even several years to achieve. The child must slowly be taken through positive naturalistic development into the higher and more socialized language development so that his personality can eventually emerge in an integrated way.

A second syndrome of behavioral deviancy is found in children who have come from homes where there has been a positive and nurturing environment but a lack of effective language and social development. This child is the *"naturalized-unsocialized"* child and represents one of the Alpha children. This child is a very creative child who enjoys much solitary activity devoid of the usual social interaction needs. This child is not unlike the primitive-unsocialized child, except that the quality and nature of early environment was dramatically different.

The naturalized child appears to disregard social rules though he is not particularly negative or hostile to peers or adults. Instead, the naturalized child is a child who enjoys all of the capabilities of right minded thinking. He is impulsive but not purposefully destructive or defensive. He usually enjoys much active play and is often very physical with other children, sometimes hurting them accidentally though the adult often sees this behavior as intentional. The natural-unsocialized child communicates physically and nonverbally. He may hit other children or hurt them in a playful way in an attempt to relate to them. He simply does not "think" of talking or learning to relate in normal ways. When he is reprimanded for some infraction of the rules he will often withdraw, engage in thumbsucking or pouting, and appear more hurt and confused than angry.

The naturalized child is often overly protected at home and few structured demands are placed on his behavior. He does not have to learn specific social behaviors at home because the parents are either unable to place limits on his behavior or, in some cases, because the parents are attempting, in a misguided way, to raise their child in an environment of open and overly accepting behavior between adult and child. It is even possible that some exceptionally bright children who have high abilities in right mindedness but much lower abilities in left mindedness also exhibit these characteristics. Due to the depressed capabilities in language processing, the child engages in the more natural behavior since it gives more pleasure and feelings of positive self-concept.

The naturalized-unsocialized child is one who must learn social expectations and the use of language as a mediator in behavior. The earlier such a child is placed with other children the more likely he will learn language and social behaviors. During the kindergarten year these children are often seen as immature and even excluded from kindergarten as a means of giving them more time for the natural process of maturity. Unfortunately, these children need more experience not less during these early years. Not only should this child be in kindergarten, but he should be in an all day program under the guidance of a sensitive teacher who can give him the sorts of experiences which will assure appropriate social development. If these children are left to their own maturation rate it is likely that their socialized behaviors will continue to be repressed under the more ego-centered naturalistic interests.

If the naturalized-unsocialized child is not given assistance early, he may become even more difficult to integrate into social groups. He may become negative and develop extreme feelings of rejection and incompetence. This usually results in eventual aggressive behavior, just as in the case of the primitive and unsocialized child. Again, this child needs language and social experiences early just as does the primitive child.

We all have much more in common with both the primitive-unsocialized and natural-unsocialized child than we may care to know. One characteristic of the naturalized child is his tendency to utilize right minded thinking as a primary mode of perception and consciousness. All of us may experience such a world in the unseen world of our dreams. It is thought that much of our control and involvement in many forms of dreaming is in the realm of right hemispheric function. In dreams we can take flight on our fantasies, reliving pleasurable events or solving problems which have plagued us during waking hours. Our solutions may be unrealistic such as flying about above all of the confusion and pressures of the day or assuming the role of king over a kingdom which follows our every bidding. The world of dreams is similar to the creative ability which we can often bring to the fore during consciousness. In creativity we often discover unique solutions, novel ways of meeting new situations, or the visualization of extended possibilities in reaching our goals. In consciousness our creative ability is a synthesis of the unchained and fantasy-oriented right mindedness with the order and logic of our left mindedness. But scattered research has shown in certain forms of sleep that the interconnectedness between the hemispheres is "blocked" so that the right hemisphere assumes free will and expression without the moral and logical control of the left hemisphere.

When we experience the often chaotic and yet uncontrolled creativity of the right hemisphere during sleep, we are to some degree experiencing a bit of the world of the naturalistic child. He has little regard for time and sequence, cause and effect, or the logical relationships in his new environment. He responds with naturalistic thought to sensory information about him without mediation from socialized thinking. If the child is a primitive child he has not learned socialized behaviors and therefore must respond to his environment much as we do in dreams. He has difficulty seeing relationships, in predicting what will happen as a consequence of his behavior, or organizing himself so that predictable outcomes will occur. Each event in his life is a singular happening monitored only by previous learning relative to unmediated and conditioned responses. If adults have often treated him cruelly or denied the love and security he needed, he learns to respond "automatically" to adult behavior with anxiety and a lack of trust.

With the primitive child we must slowly replace conditioned responses with new experiences and new expectations, first through physical and loving interaction and then with language to identify and relate such experiences to the organization of left hemisphere learning. This takes much time, and if it is not begun early we may find increasing difficulty in making the needed changes. The child will be caught endlessly in a frightening and unpredictable world.

In the case of the naturalistic child, there is more potential for change for he has learned some socialized thinking but "prefers" the more naturalistic mode of consciousness. It may be that in both of these children some minor neurological difficulty exists in the interconnectedness between the two hemispheres so that the process of psychosynthesis is never complete, or at least inefficient; thus, the right hemisphere continues to control consciousness even during waking. But the naturalized child is able, through external controls and assistance, to learn the socialized processes and can eventually bring a more integrated function to consciousness. Many artists and creative individuals who continue to have difficulties with social learning may be our naturalistic child grown into adulthood. The individual does learn social convention and values but finally rejects them in favor of his dominant right minded view of the world. However, not all creative or artistic individuals remain at odds with the values and social structures of the culture. In many cases, an individual with strong right mindedness may adhere to and even enjoy the socialized world about him. Such an individual may become interested in many fields of medicine, building trades, mechanical trades, or simply arts and crafts in which both socialized and naturalized thought can be given acceptable expression. For such an individual, naturalized thought may continue to make him somewhat verbally and socially inept, but he will still enjoy being with people and gaining their acceptance and praise. The naturalistic individual who neither learns nor accepts social values may remain a critic of society and either live an isolated and bohemian life or remain on the edge of acceptability while using his art form to express his disdain for society. He might enter a field of research in the biological or natural sciences where he can study and learn about nature while gaining the advantages of living a socially acceptable life. In this way the naturalized individual, as opposed to the primitive individual, may be able to use his natural mode of personality to gain a place in society. The primitive individual may continue to have much difficulty in society due to his inability to develop and use language or socialized thought.

This short discussion suggests that there is at least another major way of looking at behavioral deviance in these two basic types of behavioral syndromes other than simply looking at such individuals as being "disturbed," "eccentric," or in some way as an individual who is a deviant and who needs treatment. Teachers and parents can effect significant changes in both types of children, not so much by altering their behavior toward a totally acceptable form as by attempting to educate them and also accept some of their behavior as a different but acceptable way to be. Initially, much of the behavior of these children is seen as so different from other children that the adult becomes alarmed and labels the child as sick, learning disabled, or brain damaged. This sort of reaction has the effect of further alienating the child and forcing him into his naturalistic mode of personality to protect himself. Nature makes many different kinds of children; society determines if the product is acceptable or not by its own self-imposed value structure. For many of these children the problem is not that they are inherently bad or incompetent; it is, rather, a question of how much variation we are willing to accept in the way of humanity. It is interesting to note that some of the most creative and productive individuals in history in the fields of art, music, science, and philosophy have been individuals who found the social structure of their time inappropriate and archaic. They were often rejected for their strangeness before the culture realized that they were men and women of genius who were naturalistic and creative people. This historical reflection suggests that we must never be too quick to attempt to place everyone in the plastic bag of "normal" as a means of evaluating a person's worth. Certainly, when a child, potentially competent or not, exhibits behavior which is destructive to those about him, then intervention must occur. Yet, teachers must assure that a child's behavioral "problem" is not created solely by the teacher's rigidity, limitations, and expectations. If

so, we risk including capable but different children from participation in society.

Most importantly, the notion of looking at undisciplined
behavior as a learning deficit, rather than as some sort of undefinable personality disorder, will put the adult in the conceptual stance of developing effective learning and instructional
environments rather than attempting a clinical diagnosis or
treatment which will solve a "problem."

Education and socialization are both left hemispheric processes. Education is left minded! Since all children do not come
equally balanced in left and right minded potential, it is obvious that many children will be seen as undisciplined and
chaotic simply because they do not "think" the same way as
teachers. Education is the process of teaching the left mind to
gain control of the neuro-system in the form of factual information and socialized behavior. This process of training the
left hemisphere to become dominant, as we have discussed earlier, begins during the first year of life and even during the first
few days. We cannot take exception with this process for it is
important that the child learn the nature of his culture and the
discipline of language and values in order to eventually develop a high level of personal psychosynthesis. But it appears
that much of our Western culture is so embued with an intense
desire to socialize everyone that we often teach left minded
thinking to the detriment of the naturalistic part of our beings.
Children can become so engrained with logic, values, reason,
time, and order that they become mechanistic and unable to
express the creative and natural aspect of their mind. This can
lead to individuals who are unable to think creatively and who
must find a logical reason for all activity. The highly technological individual may be unable to recognize that the very
nature of his socialized mind and societal pressure is the basis
for the eventual deterioration of his physical capacities through
heart attacks, nutritional deficiencies, gastrointestinal disorders, and the pain of low back stress. The naturalistic part of
our being needs exercise, movement and physical expression,
and the freshness of expressing one's being in an open natural
way. The naturalistic child often grows up while his tutors

grow old.

The educational curriculum should be developed so that children are also taught in right minded functions as well as the left and usual mode of thought. The young infant, prior to the end of the first year, learns most significantly through his eyes, through movement, touch, taste, and smell. During the early part of the second year through the early part of the third year, the child learns at a rapid pace, incorporating more and more information into his ever expanding language structure. As mentioned earlier, it is during this period of time that much of the child's adult potential and personality structure may be set. This is the earliest period of psychosynthesis during which both the naturalized and socialized learning are being integrated. During this period the parent must provide opportunity for exploration, response to the child's curiosity and experimentation but not to the point of preventing the child's natural learning, and an environment in which the child can accumulate information and experience in a secure and loving atmosphere.

When the first days of formal education begin around the ages of four to five years, the child enters the next stage of rapid psychosynthesis potential. From this point on the teacher must provide, just as the parent did following the first year, an environment of security and endless opportunity for exploration. This environment ought to be structured to assure language learning and a continuance of the natural experiences of the child. The child must constantly find new thoughts and experiences to explore; he must be "involved" in them; and he must incorporate them into language and organize his experience with language skills. This pattern, naturalistic involved learning followed by evaluation and language integration, is the most effective way for children to learn. First, learning is concrete and experiential; then it is ordered, related, and abstracted through language. One cannot grow plants of wisdom without first planting seeds of experience. We speak of this process vaguely in education and even refer to exploratory learning but the educational version is far removed from the actual developmental and natural phenomenon upon which the theory is based. As more and more experience is gained, the developing abstractions can eventually be utilized to create experience. But this process does not occur until years of experiences and abstractions are known and integrated. It may even be suspected that the true consciousness of all being is rooted not in our logic and language but there in our earliest being, the naturalistic and right mindedness of our soul. What may frighten and frustrate us so about the naturalistic child, the Alpha child, is not so much his lack of social ability but his reminder, sometimes not so gentle a reminder at that, of our own naturalistic yearnings.

The primitive-unsocialized child, while operating in a naturalistic mode of thought, is often a child who has had so much abuse and deprivation that both verbal and nonverbal capabilities are seriously impaired. We have alluded to the probable difficulty in socializing this child, and it can be recognized that both early intervention and long term specialized schooling may be required. But the highly naturalized child who has not had so much abuse and who may exhibit significant social development which is most often deferred in favor of naturalized function is a child with whom the school can often make significant progress if some understanding is gained of his needs.

One child who illustrated the naturalized syndrome was brought to the office because his teacher had become frustrated in attempts to teach him or deal with his constant interruptions in class. Gerald was an active ten-year-old who had been to several clinics, the most recent being a large medical center program. He had been diagnosed as hyperactive, of course, and he was. He had also had the privilege of being diagnosed as "dyslexic" which had made him somewhat of a hero about the house in that the parents felt he had some dread disease from which he might recover only after a great deal of time and then only partially. This had been effective, at least, in assuring his parents solicitious cooperation so that he could engage in his favorite pastimes of building things, painting a large dinosaur on the bathroom wall colorfully done in his mother's favorite lipstick, and leaving the family cat in a homemade rocket slated for blastoff sometime in the spring. Fortunately, the cat was saved from space and sought another family, but Gerald remained.

The most recent "evaluation" of Gerald had given the school and the family their first clue to Gerald's needs, but neither the school nor the family had made much sense of it. The evaluation had cleared Gerald of his dylexia condition and had stated that he had no learning disability at all, but rather was very bright with a significant difference between verbal and nonverbal intelligence. Gerald was an Alpha child! Gerald had a habit of socking kids in the hallway, bothering them during seat work, and generally creating havoc in the lunchroom. Discipline usually consisted of rather lengthy threats and lectures on the virtues of learning to read and leaving everyone else alone. He had difficulty attending to his work, daydreamed a great deal, continued to write illegibly, avoided listening to anything said to him, and, apparently, purposefully tested the very limits of school. Gerald did win first prize for his Halloween creation in the form of a space robot with magnificently arrayed blinking lights and whirling objects placed all about and manipulated from inside.

The morning he wore it to school, he was not allowed on the bus, whereupon his mother took him to school with robot in arm. However, before he entered the school he was able to put on his creation and enter the building, terrorizing the entire kindergarten class just prior to their "show and tell" period which he disrupted by entering the room presumably by mistake. The larger part of the morning he sat in the principal's office buzzing and blinking the school secretary into distraction until the principal returned from an early morning meeting in the central office. But, he did get first prize for his Halloween costume, notwithstanding the havoc caused by his arrival in the community sometime that morning. The family did have to replace their Christmas tree lights when he refused to return them since "Robot-A" needed them the remainder of the year as it stood condemned to a corner of his room.

I listened sympathetically to the parents as they related their world to me. Gerald's nonverbal intelligence emerged as gifted, while his total verbal output fell into the just average range. Gerald's saving characteristic was that he had never become socialized enough to feel that there might be something "wrong" with him and he was spared from the feelings of guilt and "dumbness" that many Alpha children come to feel as they find themselves in constant conflict with the population of this strange planet upon which they must have been accidentally born. Gerald's mother had become fond, it seemed, of stating that she and her husband were never meant to be parents.

After some discussion the parents began to feel at least a little more worthy. It was found that Gerald had learned to read and in fact, on a short test without writing requirements, he was able to read at grade level and comprehended what he read. But there were problems, including his tendency to fatigue early while reading, making it impossible for him to follow an assignment for any period of time before turning to his daydreams as a means of reliving both the boredom and frustration of reading. At one time he had been evaluated by a visual specialist since, like many parents today, Gerald's parents felt that he might have a "perceptual problem" which had been cited in a recent popular magazine as being an "unnoticed" learning disability in many children. He had been diagnosed as having a rather severe acuity problem which required lens correction. Unfortunately, after a brief period of time both at home and school when it was expected that everything would be better, he continued to display the same difficulties as before. He did look "smarter" though and many of the children appeared more sympathetic toward him. Gerald for the most part never seemed to care much either way about his glasses. It did improve his building coordination and that pleased him so he wore them.

Deviant Socialized Behavior

Just as children may develop overly naturalized behaviors which reach the limits of acceptable personality characteristics, so may children develop in overly socialized patterns. In that normal socialization provides the neuro-structure for development of language, values, order, and reason, an overemphasis in this area of competency can produce children who exhibit characteristics based on the extremes of such competencies.

There are many possibilities for the development of dominant and extremely socialized thought processes. As might be expected, since this is the desired pattern at normal levels of competency, the school and standard middle class families tend to produce children with behavioral deviancy in this manner. Aside from potential nutritional, metabolic, or neurological dysfunctions in the right hemisphere which might give the left hemisphere added importance, there are a great number of functional and learning environments which may produce the overly socialized child. The latter concerns are our focus in the following discussion.

One child most susceptible to the high left minded syndrome is the child who has innate capacities in left hemispheric function which are superior to the right potential. Even though a child may have genetic predisposition toward high verbal skills, the environment can increase it by either reinforcing this capacity or by creating it artificially through conditioning and experience.

One of the earliest conditions which may predispose the infant to overly socialized function can be that of the highly verbal and moralistic mother. If the parent is overly concerned with cleanliness, with appropriate standards of behavior, and with gaining social acceptance for both her and her child, then the stage is set for creating the highly socialized child. Such a mother will tend to provide experiences for the child which give the child feedback as to his acceptance as a social being. This can begin early with the mother being overly attentive and concerned about the child's behavior and welfare. The mother's anxiety and concern for the safety of the child during the first two years can communicate anxiety and caution to the child. His naturalistic tendencies toward exploration and experimentation will be thwarted by mother's constant attention and restriction on his behavior. This will often be followed by verbal warnings and nonverbal implications of danger or even unacceptability. Such a child will not experience the exploratory and experimenting behaviors so important in giving him a growing feeling of independence and curiosity. He will remain close to his mother and seek her superior strength in order to assure security. The child will remain closely attached and identified with his mother as his alter ego and protector. He will remain dependent upon the mother and unable to trust his own capacities. Such a child will tend toward conforming behaviors in which language comes to play a significant role early in life.

This continued dependence upon mother will foster a strong and important emotional relationship between the child and mother which may be seen by others as a loving relationship. The child may be highly obedient and observe behaviors which gain him continued acceptance and love from his mother. This close and yet dependent relationship will be one in which early language and formal learning can be developed. The child attends to behavioral rules and, subsequently, to values much earlier than other children. It is possible that the child even becomes anxious when he fears he may do something wrong even though this is not the case.

Many of these children become quite manipulative and possessive of the closest playmate and the mother. This possessiveness can take two major directions; the child demands the mother's attention because he is fearful about losing her security, or he continues to be so ego-centered that he desires to control his environment. Some children can develop both of these characteristics and become demanding and yet anxious children. The child learns language and social behavior early and is denied the natural development in exploration and experimentation which would stimulate naturalistic skills. By the time the child reaches the age of five and is ready to enter school this pattern of neurological organization and personality characteristics can be quite pervasive and difficult to change. We might call this child the opposite of the Alpha child, or the Theta child. The Theta child is a socially and verbally active child who thrives on the social need structure of the culture.

If the Alpha child is the soul of the culture, the Theta child is its technology. These two children represent the two positions of man, socialized and technological, and naturalized and intuitive. They are the poles of personality structure in the normal human being. The naturalized child is physically active and often unable to organize himself within time, but the Theta child is overly concerned with time and finds some difficulty in developing adequate physical and spatial organization. The natural child cannot remember the name of the day while the socialized child knows all of the names, even though he may not truly understand them. One child is blessed with the ability to name everything but finds that it makes little "sense," while the other makes "sense" out of everything and knows no names at all.

Few children are totally socialized or solely naturalistic, but our concern is when dominance in one direction or the other tends to depress the alternate function. Some degree of hemispheric difference is perhaps unavoidable, but when the degree of difference affects a child's total level of psychosynthesis capacity then intervention is required. The overly socialized child may find it difficult to function without definite guidelines in both social and learning behaviors. As he grows away from the proximity of his mother's overseeing abilities, he must find substitutes for the direction, support, and security that mother provided and which he has never learned for himself. Social values of behavior in the school and the careful learning of facts and knowledge supply the needed substitutes, and the child becomes a compulsive achiever.

The Theta child has basic personality imperatives to become highly socialized and achievement oriented in school. Competition, nearly unknown to the Alpha child, becomes a frantic fixation for this child though he may claim he learns only because "it's the right thing to do." The Theta child feels lost without definite guidelines and rules followed by some sort of social indication that he is to be rewarded. The rewards in the usual educational environment are definite and varied in the form of teacher praise, acceptance, grades, social status, special privileges and opportunities, and academic advancement. It is the Theta child who gives so much pleasure to the parent and teacher who themselves need to demonstrate their own worthiness as parents and teachers — the adult Thetas. The cost for the Theta child is mental health, sensitivity, wonder and curiosity, and spontaneity, all of which must be sacrificed in favor of security and acceptance. We must remember that the socialized characteristics are desirable ends in learning, though in the Theta child they may become neurotic behavioral extremes. There is sadness not only for the loss of soul in these individuals but for the nearly devastating effects upon the wondering Alpha child who finds himself in their world.

The highly socialized behavior and personality of the Theta child is not in itself deviant, but his motivation for behaving in this manner is a matter of concern. Most children have a mixture of socialized and naturalized interests and personality characteristics. The Theta child, aside from being overly concerned with achievement and social acceptance, often develops difficulties in naturalized competencies through neglect. The Theta child, in his desire for achievement and social acceptance, often becomes obsessed with winning, being first, gaining all of the attention of adults, being the first in line, the best reader, and engaging in many behaviors which are so competitive that other children reject him. This obsessive compulsive behavior is a misguided attempt to substitute security from the environment for the lack of internal independence which was not established during those early years. As many adult neurotics come to discover, we cannot always replace early childhood deprivation through alternate behavioral strategies. Mother is gone forever once we pass the moment when she is needed and no amount of compensation or rationalization can ever bring us the infant love and security which was lost so long ago. If the teacher discovers this syndrome early, she can alter the child's behavior and his neurotic obsession with socialization. She can do this by increasing his naturalized behavioral interests and activities and providing social reinforcement not just for socialized competencies but for naturalized competencies as well. The teacher must be alert to these needs, for the usual curriculum does not include much in the way of naturalization reinforcement.

When the teacher or parent is able to give social reinforcement, which the child desires, and to encourage nonverbal and naturalized learning, the child may then begin to structure those poorly developed self-concept structures which were not nurtured in early life. More will be said about curricula for right minded children in later chapters.

The concept of hemispheric differences as a basis for personality disorders is a different way of looking at the behavior of children. While there are distinctive and well-established personality syndromes which indicate emotional disturbance in children, this viewpoint provides a broader consideration for those concerned with mental health. Deviancy, in itself, does not necessarily indicate a mental state which can be described as "disturbed." Deviancy only implies that an individual "deviates" from the normal expected patterns of behavior for children of a particular age. The overly naturalized or socialized child presents a deviant behavioral pattern. These patterns, as has been pointed out, are based on a variety of genetic, cultural, and learning factors. Children who are different in their general hemispheric organization need not be disturbed but certainly, like any other individual, children with a different pattern of hemispheric organization may also be disturbed. The matter of actual disturbance must be diagnosed by competent mental health professionals. Yet, the information here should encourage mental health personnel to expand their concept of normal behavior and to avoid labelling hemispherically different children as disturbed merely because they exhibit a deviant personality pattern. A major difference between the hemispherically different child who is also disturbed and the child without disturbance is that the latter will be receptive to learning alternate behavioral strategies which can allow for school adjustment without mental health intervention. This distinction will need to be made through educational and mental health intervention.

Chapter 6

RECOGNITION OF CEREBRAL STYLES OF DOMINANCE

IN the preceding chapters we have discussed general concepts and developing theories concerning cerebral dominance. It is important to realize that there are many variables involved in such theories and that too little is known to formulate clear and scientifically based constructs. As has been pointed out in the beginning of the book, the reader is encouraged to consider the theories presented here as tentative and open to the reader's own experience and experimentation. Even with the increased research, knowledge of neurological function in the central nervous system remains a new frontier in human behavior. For the educator and the psychologist who must infer relationships between behavior and neurological development, a great deal of caution and professional experience must be brought to bear when applying tentative research findings to children in school.

Yet, as often happens, any new or promising theory which appears potentially valuable or may assist in understanding child development and learning may be grasped and used with little understanding. The following discussion may provide a framework on which the teacher and psychologist can build personal direction for future research and for applying tentative constructs concerning hemisphericity to children in school. The information presented here is given with the expectation that professionals will apply it in reasonable ways and with caution. If the constructs provide at least a general change for the better in the orientation of teaching methods, then our purpose will be served. Perhaps the greatest difficulty in applying the cerebral dominance theory is that the professional must consider many possibilities and select those which demonstrate practical value. If this is done, then much of what is to follow can have immediate and important implications in working with children.

If the foregoing information is to have impact, then some guidelines must be developed with which the psychologist and the teacher can identify cerebral dominance styles in children.

Children use naturalistic right minded approaches, or socialized left minded approaches to learning due to neurological difference or competence, for a number of cultural and personal reasons. Our first step is to recognize when the responses of children imply a tendency toward preference for naturalistic or socialized thought. Such preference in itself is not so important as whether it prevents the child from learning effectively and whether that preference can be modulated to include both styles of perception and behavior. If a child demonstrates a strong preference for one or the other mode of functioning with great resistance to change, then we must attempt to continually stimulate the deficit process while teaching through the major preference. The first problem is to determine whether a preference exists and particularly whether that preference is naturalistic or right minded. If this is the case, there are many learning and behavioral factors which need understanding and attention.

Wechsler Intelligence Scale for Children — Revised

In the clinical setting the psychologist has many opportunities to measure hemisphericity preferences with psychometric instruments. The WISC-R Intelligence test is one of the most widely used psychometric instruments in the measurement of the intelligence of children. The test is utilized with children ages six through sixteen years with other forms of the test available for children under six years and adults. The test is divided into two different series of test items, one yielding a verbal intelligence score and the other yielding a performance intelligence score. There are six subtests used in evaluating verbal intelligence and six utilized in the performance section. The verbal tests include items relating to associative thinking and general information, common sense and reasoning, basic arithmetical concepts, abstract and concrete reasoning abilities,

understanding of words, and ability to utilize auditory information in proper sequence. The performance test includes the
ability to visualize essential from nonessential detail, ability to
see a total situation based on verbal comprehension, ability to
perceive, analyze, synthesize, and reproduce abstract designs,
visual motor coordination and simple assembly skills, overall
psychomotor ability, and ability to use foresight and planning
in a visual motor task.[1]

Investigators have found that when individuals with evidence
of brain impairment are given the WISC-R, those with impairment in the left hemisphere do better on the performance part
of the test than on the verbal. Those whose impairment seems
to be in the right hemisphere do better with verbal skills.[2] Such
research has often pointed to this difference and is suggestive
that the verbal subtests relate more to left hemispheric function
while performance subtests relate more to right hemispheric
function. Our own experience with the WISC-R also supports
this concept. However, most of the research heretofore has
looked at this data as indicative of some sort of hemispheric
dysfunction rather than the other viewpoint: one hemisphere
may provide more efficient processing for a child while the
lesser hemisphere need not particularly display some sort of
neurological deficit. For example, a child with a great difference in the two IQ scores may display an IQ of 95 in the verbal
abilities but 130 in the performance abilities. In the typical
deficit viewpoint it is assumed that there is some sort of neurological problem particularly in the verbal hemisphere. In our
work we have found that often children with this sort of difference do not particularly display any actual deficit in verbal
abilities but merely that they display higher competence in the
nonverbal or performance abilities. In this example, if the child
displays additional difficulties relating to language and communication, then an analysis of neurological difficulties may
be substantiated. But when we look at such differences from the
potential viewpoint of cerebral dissonance it is suggested not
that there is a neurological deficit but simply a difference
which has the effect of altering the child's general perceptual
and learning style.

In final analysis, should one take the neurological deficit

viewpoint or the cerebral dissonance approach, the treatment for the child still remains one of educational and behavioral formulations and not some sort of medical treatment. If there are no indicators of brain dysfunction which might respond to medication or surgery, then it matters little that the child has a neurological dysfunction. It is just as reasonable and more appropriate to assume a cerebral dissonance viewpoint — which tends to be more positive and useful in educational planning since both viewpoints, in the absence of dysfuncton responsive to medical treatment, must take essentially an educational remediation approach. The authors were once present in a situation concerning medical diagnosis of minimal brain dysfunction which has implications to this discussion. For some time a medical center in the area where the authors practiced had been doing research with children described as minimally brain damaged. Schools had referred great numbers of children suspected of minimal brain dysfunction. The school's officials hoped to obtain a diagnosis of the condition and, obviously, some sort of medical intervention in the disorder which would allow the child to learn. At one point, following many frustrations in meeting the needs of these children, one of the chief neurologists explained to a school official that in most cases children referred did have various types of minimal brain dysfunction but that this condition was primarily an educational problem and not a medical issue. It took some time for the school officials to understand the implications of this statement. The neurologist explained that since little could be done to alter the condition medically the real problem was how the school would teach the child even though he had minimal brain dysfunction. The problem was one of learning and development and not medical intervention. He explained that other than some indicators of how the child might best learn there was little that the medical field had to offer with their diagnosis except in those rare cases where some medication might provide temporary relief from some of the symptoms.

In summary, many investigators have found high correlations between left hemispheric function and verbal tasks on the WISC-R and right hemispheric function and performance tasks. We have found this to be true, particularly when the psychologists look at specific subtest tasks and learning or behavioral components of the child's responses. The diagnosis of hemispheric dissonance or hemispheric dysfunction is difficult at best but it does provide a new perspective to utilizing a well-known psychometric instrument.

Comparison of Verbal and Performance Scores on the WISC-R

In much of the literature on the WISC-R Intelligence Test it is often assumed that children with a significant difference between the verbal and performance portions are demonstrating potential emotional disturbance or neurological dysfunction. In both cases, relative to the naturalistic child, this may be true behaviorally but untrue in the sense that there is actual disturbance or dysfunction. We may be dealing with difference in hemisphericity which results in syndromes of behavior characteristic of emotional difficulties or neurological dysfunction but which are in fact "normal" for this particular child. Yet, if the child does not display a significant number of clinical indicators toward hemisphericity, then the difference may indicate the typical disturbance or dysfunction syndrome. The verbal items on the WISC are basically left hemisphere oriented while the performance items, though they require some language, are primarily right hemisphere oriented.

Much research has been done concerning the clinical indicators of specific subtests as related to various neurological functions. From a psychoneurological viewpoint, the generalization that the two major areas of the WISC can be so easily designated as left or right hemisphere related would be unacceptable. Our purpose here is not to imply that complex neurological functions can be separated so easily, but to suggest that a more global viewpoint be assumed than the usual specificity applied to particular functions of WISC responses. Further, in looking in a general way at hemisphericity preference, it is somewhat simplified to assume that there is at least a general tendency toward significant differences in global scores for the two WISC classifications of language and performance tests. There are often many discrepancies in the general language or performance scores as indicators of right or left hemisphere preference. General scores with at least a fifteen point difference between language and performance items is one indicator of a potential hemisphere preference. In many cases the two major scores did not display a fifteen point difference but there was a cluster of other indicators of hemisphere preference. In such cases it may be found that the two scores are quite similar and yet many of the following indicators may be found to definitely indicate a hemisphere preference. Thus, though a child may display similar competence in both language and performance items, there may still be significant hemisphere preference. In such a case equal competence in language and performance abilities provides the child with potential equalized preference but this potential is not utilized and a distinct preference exists for reasons other than basic neurological competency.

The use of language and performance test differences as a single indicator then is not valid. This is true with all of the following indicators. The diagnostician cannot use one indicator to make a hemisphericity diagnosis, but must utilize several indicators and his own professional experience to make the difficult analysis of hemisphere preference. Several indicators utilized during the evaluation will often provide a rather substantial body of information to suggest the hemisphere preference if one truly exists.

Differential Motivational Response on the WISC

One of the most significant indicators of hemisphere preference toward the naturalized orientation has been a difference in the child's motivational response to performance items in comparison to language items. The evaluator may often see the child struggle with language items while showing a distinct preference and increased interest during performance items. Often the child may give one word response to information, similarity, or vocabulary items and then give very directed and sophisticated responses to the picture completion, block design, picture arrangement, and object assembly items. It is often significant that during performance items the child can be seen making predictive responses to performance items while even poor language responses require much thought and eventual short and inadequate answers. For example, many children tend to move the blocks about on block design, seeming to test out various possibilities. The Alpha child will often look at the design, study the blocks momentarily, and then immediately form the design with the blocks. This behavior suggests internal imagery manipulation with subsequent clear placement of the blocks. The same is true of the picture arrangement and object assembly. This difference between language imagery and spatial imagery (while formulating responses) is a clear indication of hemispheric preference. Usually, such a difference not only results in higher scores on performance items than on the language items, but other indicators will also be present to verify the naturalistic tendency.

Characteristics of the Alpha Child

Imagery Projection

The apparent ability to use visual imagery, as described above, on performance items of the WISC is indicative of a high degree of right hemisphere competence. The difference between this sort of imagery production and that seen with language items suggests differential efficiency between the hemispheres. In these cases, manipulation of spatial information appears more easily accomplished by the child than manipulation of verbal-spatial information such as in language items. The evaluator has to be alert to the motivation features of these two styles of response for this is not an area that can be scored easily and goes beyond the standardization of the test. Often, due to concern for standardization and scoring, an examiner may miss this subtle and significant indicator during the test. Similar differences can be seen in the classroom as the child deals with verbal items or tasks, as compared with more spatially oriented tasks. This will become clear as the following indicators are reviewed.

Difficulties in Specific Recall

The examiner gives the child the verbal items in the standardized manner and records the scores. Then, the examiner again gives the verbal items allowing the child to select from alternate answers. While the second set of questions is not included in the actual WISC scoring, the purpose is to gain some understanding of the child's recall potential when given concrete cues.

The Alpha child is spatially oriented and is prone to recognize verbal material but to have difficulty recalling material without definite available choices. On the language subtest involving information the child is asked questions which require specific recall. Often the naturalistic child will be unable to remember specific verbal facts but be able to recognize the correct response if given a multiple choice including the correct response. Just as the verbal child may be able to efficiently recall vast amounts of verbal data, so may the naturalistic child be able to recognize spatial or verbal responses from concrete alternatives.

Syntax Difficulties on the WISC

Often the naturalistic child has difficulty formulating verbal responses in a proper syntax. This may be seen on vocabulary and similarities subtests. The examiner will note a number of typical naturalized responses. It should be remembered that the naturalistic child *knows* the response but is unable to organize it in appropriate language. He may stammer out a disorganized verbal response which includes the correct answer, but the language production is often syntactically incorrect. For example, in response to "How are an apple and a banana alike?" the child answers "You both eat them." Similarly, he responds to "How are beer and wine alike?" with "You both drink them." On vocabulary he may respond to the meaning of gamble with, "Play, you money, its a game." Such responses may indicate difficulty in speech production or articulation, but when combined with several naturalistic indicators they may also imply that the child is having difficulty translating global naturalistic impressions into an organized verbal response.

Simple Verbal Responses

The naturalistic child tends to think of holistic images. To give a well-articulated response when one thinks in entire images is quite difficult. Children who have limited verbal ability often give one word responses to such questions as "What is the meaning of 'gamble'?" So do many of the naturalistic children. These children often become quite sophisticated in selecting one word to convey an entire thought. Thus, in response to the word "gamble" the examiner may get "money-game." Further questioning by the examiner will usually distinguish between the verbally limited child and the naturalistic child who understands the word but is unable or unwilling to use all of the language needed to make a well articulated response.

Difficulty in Arithmetical Computation

The naturalistic child may not think logically though he is capable. Math can be difficult for him and, due to his tendency to visualize information, he has difficulty using symbols to represent numbers. The Alpha child often continues to rely on his fingers or other concrete objects to provide the basis for computation. Needless to say, the Alpha child often does poorly on the arithmetic subtest of the WISC and generally is a slower student in the classroom in this area. While he may master the mathematical facts, story problems, algebra or higher math become a great mystery.

Person and Picture Drawing

Often, though not always, the Alpha child likes to draw because his world is populated with visual images and he has a need to reconstruct or communicate his fantasy in concrete forms.

When asked to draw a picture, the naturalistic child will do so, should he wish to, with some vigor and interest. His pictures will often contain the elaborations of the creative and imaginative child that he is. There will often be action, elaboration in the forms and specific details of the person or object, and detailed backgrounds. The child who has equally socialized and naturalized ability will ask the examiner exactly what sort of drawing the examiner wants, while the naturalized child will prefer his own and usually will not ask but simply begin the task in his own way. It should be remembered, though, that the naturalistic child often does not like to follow directions and may attempt to draw as simple a drawing as possible simply to satisfy the examiner. After asking the child to draw some specific picture, of a person, for example, at a later point in the session, the examiner may want to give the child some crayons and invite him to draw anything he wishes to. At this point one may be surprised to see a much more elaborate production than when the child is given specific directions.

Psychologists often miss much of the potential of the naturalistic child when they do not meet him on his own terms. The naturalistic child is highly sensitive to nonverbal communication and also resistive to structured situations. For this reason the entire nature of the typical psychiatric or psychological examination with convention and standardization threatens the naturalistic child, and he may respond very poorly in a manner that is not at all indicative of his true ability. In many cases the naturalistic child will purposefully given erroneous responses or unusual ones to tease or to display negative feelings about the test situation. It is very important, therefore, that the examiner have examples of the child's classroom and home activities to compare with the test situation. Of course, a sensitive examiner can usually avoid such problems and gain an adequate response to the testing.

Fine Motor Organization

The naturalistic child, as was pointed out in earlier discussions, often has unusual motoric organization including mixed dominance, directional difficulties, and organizational problems in school work. These problems are rarely manifested in the child's chosen activities, but appear when the child is asked to conform to convention and produce letters, drawings, or work which must be completed according to predetermined rules of learning.

The naturalistic child may often pay little attention to left to right organization due either to a lack of language structure or to right hemisphere dominance in motor control resulting in the typical confusion related to left handedness. While the child may not be left-handed, if the right hemisphere is the dominant control center for motor behavior, the child may tend to organize right to left. As the child develops he may compensate for directional confusion by avoiding either the left-right organization or right-left. This can be done in several ways including organizing forms and information in a vertical fashion. On the Berry Developmental Test of Visual-Motor Integration or on the Purdue Perceptual Motor Survey, the child may place the forms vertically on the page rather than across the page as is usually the case. Again, a left-handed child or a child with directional confusion who is not particularly naturalistic may also compensate for directional confusion in this manner. This reemphasizes the need to evaluate carefully, looking for several naturalistic indicators rather than assuming that this one behavior indicates a naturalistically oriented child. The naturalistic child, rather than having a learning disability, often compensates in this manner simply because it is easier for him. It is a preference rather than a need. The child usually is able to orient in a left to right fashion but does not remember to do so when absorbed in a spatial-visual task.

Some naturalistic children will simply place the forms all over the page in no particular order at all. This is very common with the naturalistic child since he is more concerned with each form in itself than with the organization of the total task.

Poor Hand Dominance or Motor Dominance Difficulties

Often, due to the conflicting relationships between cerebral and motor dominance, the naturalistic child will display poor hand dominance. He may use different hands for different tasks. In many cases the cerebral-motor dominance conflict results in difficulty in establishing clear motor dominance. The child finally learns specific tasks with the hand which, according to some internal preference, appears the most logical. This tendency inhibits the development of a specific hand dominance, and the child does not select either hand until he is faced with the left-right tasks at school. By this time there is such poor dominance that the child experiences great difficulty. In many of these children the parents often report that the child was late in establishing dominance or that he displayed much confusion about it. Since motor dominance plays a role in time orientation and general thought organization, as cited in earlier discussions, these children often display poor dominance and poor organizational or time relationships.

Lateral Hand-Body Tests

An extension of the foregoing difficulties is also noted in motor tests involving crossover commands. For example, many of these children have difficulty relating verbal directions to motor movements. If the child is asked to touch his left ear with his right hand this task often presents some difficulty though he may figure it out after some moments. In many cases the children display difficulty in kinesthetic differentiation such as being able to lift an arm and leg on opposite sides of the body when touched by the examiner.

Letter Reversals

As might be expected, many of these children have great difficulty with the proper directional orientation of letters. They also display difficulty in copying such forms as the crossed arrows on the Berry Test. When making diagonal lines, they are uncertain whether they should move up or down resulting in the typical hooks on diamonds and the arrow drawings. These children, however, are usually able to make the correct movements with a few moments of instruction and practice. This is not so with the brain-damaged child and provides another means of differentiating between the child with directional confusion as opposed to the child with actual neurological dysfunction.

Verbal Series Reversals

At the language and cognitive level, these children may often reverse the order of letters, numbers, and even words. They may remember all of the series but repeat them with some digits in reverse order. Most often these children can find their own mistakes if asked to do so, and again this assists in differentiating these children from the actual neurologically damaged children. At times these children will display difficulty in expressing themselves and will actually reverse some of their speech. They may say, "I would go like to, I mean I would like to go. . ." This often is the result of imagery thought processes in which the child is attempting to express an entire thought but is unable to maintain the thought and, at the same time, sequence his language appropriately. Often their own verbally expressed confusion creates even more confusion. As they turn their attention to the task of verbalization they may lose their thought or the expression may be a poor representation of their actual thought or its quality. This lack of visual imagery and auditory or verbal expressive integration leads teachers to feel the child is dyslexic. In many cases the child is able to perform if he is given the opportunity and if he is assisted in his verbal or auditory skills.

Visual Imagery Retention

Many of the naturalistic children, since they live in a spatial imagery world, are able to recall vividly places they have been or extensive amounts of visual imagery though they have difficulty recalling names, dates, or other verbal information associated with the imagery or experience. At times these children can remember a series of visual forms or imagery more easily than they can recall verbal information. They appear to learn more easily if there is much visual imagery attached to learning material. This is often why these children enjoy television so much. This tendency continues into adulthood, and even college students who are naturalistic-tending learn better if the professor uses much visual imagery with his lectures. The culturally deprived are often language deprived and must rely on spatial-visual information as a basis for early learning. It is not surprising then that culturally deprived children find television programs such as "Sesame Street" and "Electric Company" effective as vehicles in learning. These are often the children who are called "visual learners."

Tendency Toward Substitutions in Reading

Alpha children often make substitutions in reading and it is interesting to note that at times they make appropriate substitutions such as "river" for "stream." In this case the child internally recognizes the word as representing the visual imagery of a river, but he unconsciously substitutes the closest word that comes to mind during the "gestalt" experience of reading. One of the more common substitutions these children make, however, is that of configuration. They will often read the word "black" as "block," "when" for "what," and so forth. These are common errors when children do not attend to the actual phonetic structure of a word and are not particularly tied to a naturalistic tendency. But, when many of the other factors are present this additional factor, particularly in the older student, may indicate a tendency toward whole word gestalt rather than phonetic structure. More will be discussed concerning this problem in the section on reading difficulties.

Whole Word Retention

The naturalistic child tends to have difficulty with phonetic orientation in reading, and even after the basic sounds or units are learned each new word must still be attacked anew. Even a word which has been read in a preceding sentence may have to be read phonetically again. When not pressured by the situation though, the child will often attempt to read the whole word without using phonetics, and in cases where someone tells him the whole word he may tend to remember it more easily than in the phonetic approach. There are many complications in making an analysis of this behavior, since the tendency to remember whole word images rather than phonetic units does not indicate, in itself, a naturalistic tendency. But this tendency, when associated with a cluster of other factors, can be an important indicator. The examiner, when giving a word recognition test, can often discover such behavior.

Omissions and Incorrect Sequence in Word Recognition

Since the naturalistic child attempts to look at words holistically and also may tend to avoid proper sequence in word analysis, several common errors may be made. The child may actually read a word by seeing and saying the ending of the word first and attempt to integrate the word in a reverse fashion. For example, this difficulty can be as general as "spilt" for "split" or include the typical "was" for "saw" reversal. These difficulties occur in many children temporarily as they are first learning to read but in the naturalistic child they may even exist into adulthood. These reversals come both from the whole imagery approach and from the tendency to have difficulty in sequence or motoric directionality. At times these children will also omit words simply because in their gestalt behavior they do not visually scan nor see the actual word.

Visual Tracking and Scanning Deficits

The whole word perception tendency in these children also often creates inefficient use of the eyes. Muscles controlling the eyes are subject to the same directional preference as those controlling the hands, so that similar directional "errors" occur in visual scanning and tracking. Such children may be quick to see the most likely order of Picture Arrangement on the WISC-R and yet do very poorly on the Picture Completion. They often have difficulty with fine visual movements and may tend to avoid extensive scanning or operation of the eyes. This difficulty, combined with a tendency to perceive specific egocentric characteristics and miss important details, makes the Picture Completion task very difficult. They simply do not want to trouble themselves and often will give up easily on the fine visual motor task involving scanning. They either "see it or they don't," and they are not always willing to go through the logical and sequential visual operation of scanning. Needless to say, these children often have trouble following the sentence and then scanning back to the next sentence. They may exhibit much visual coordination difficulty and give the impression of having a visual disorder. The difficulty is not in the eye or the muscles, but in the conscious preference of the brain not to scan or sequentially investigate an object or word. This may be why many children who appear to have visual difficulties do not respond well to the typical visual training activities.

Word Calling

Word calling is a common problem with many children. They recognize the word but do not form imagery of what the word represents. For naturalistic children this is unfortunate, for they have a store of visual imagery, often richer than other children. Because they are forced to read in a phonetic sequence, they focus all of their attention upon recognition and not on imagery production. When, after reading a passage, they are asked what the passage said they are more likely to repeat the actual words, if they can remember them, than to explain the meaning of the passage. If the process is reversed, if we write down their own stories, then they are able to recall quite well. This process will be discussed in the section on reading.

Language and Automation

In earlier discussions it was pointed out that many children have difficulty in language comprehension and simultaneous motoric activity. Normally, a child develops the ability to send messages to the Automatic Sensory Motor Mechanism (where specific motoric programs are stored with resultant automatic motoric function) while thinking of some language event. In spelling the child must concentrate on the language aspects of the word while simultaneously writing the word. The ASM writes the word in an automatic fashion following messages from the language center. The focus of consciousness in this case is in the language center and "unconscious" messages are forwarded automatically to the ASM. If there are difficulties in this process then the child has to shift his attention from one mode to the other, often making errors in writing or forgetting the language component. The following three clinical signs are often indicative of this difficulty so often seen in the naturalistic child.

Finger Tapping and Language Recall

The child is asked to place both hands outstretched and flat on the table in front of him. He is asked to tap the index finger of each hand simultaneously. This task, in itself, is an indicator of lateral control in both sides of the body. If the child cannot perform this function then difficulties in bilateral control should be noted. To this task is added a language recall behavior. While the child is tapping, what should be a continuous ASM automatic function, the child is asked to repeat his phone number, his street address, or some other familiar number. The child who has difficulties in automation will stop tapping his fingers while he concentrates on the language task. Any other child will continue to tap but say the numbers in time with his finger tapping. In both cases, loss of finger tapping or tapping in time with the words or letters, the child is displaying difficulties in language and automation.

Attentional Difficulty While Performing a Task

Since these children are so motoric and spatially oriented they have difficulty in simultaneous motoric and language function. If they are working on a motoric task such as writing they may actually be unable to hear questions given to them. Conversely, as has just been illustrated, if they are engaged in a language task, they are unable to perform a simple motoric task.

Random Meandering

Random meandering has been mentioned before. It is part of the same language-automation syndrome. If the child is concentrating on a spatial-motoric task he is in good control, but when he has to attend to language he is unable to control his body and tends to appear hyperactive.

Daydreaming and Fantasy

The socialized child thinks logically and within the time and responsibility of the situation. The naturalized child tends to be creative and produce much internal imagery. Thus, the preferred mode of personal consciousness of the natural child tends to be that of fantasy and daydreaming. In this activity the child may be intensely alert and engaged in creative and fruitful problem solving. It may well not be on the expected task, but the child is as much at home in his fantasy world as is the usual child in his language world. Parents and teachers often report that this child daydreams a lot or looks out the window too often when he should be task oriented. Inquiry into this area is an important clinical indicator of the naturalistic syndrome and should not be missed by the examiner.

Forgetfulness and Absent-mindedness

We have already discussed the naturalistic child's problems with orientation to time and his engaging in much fantasy. Thus, the naturalistic child often appears to forget easily or seems to be absent minded. This is true both because of poor time orientation and due to a lack of language organization. He is often absorbed in personal imagery and does not think about time or is likely to forget easily. It is not that the child cannot remember or orient to time, for his natural thought process does not include terms of sequence and time. Following directions may be difficult, not because he cannot retain directions, but because he forgets to remember.

Orientation Toward Sensory-Motor Activity

Many naturalistic children display a high interest in a range of nonverbal activities. While any one child may display only some of the range of possible behaviors, the ones displayed not only appear to hold high interest for the child but he is usually fairly capable in such activities. These children may build, take apart, point, draw, play games, engage in musical activities, and generally love activity or active play which involves a challenge. It is not just that they enjoy activity but rather there is usually a high degree of cognitive function involved beyond simply play. It is their world and they delight in exercising what for them is a natural way to think, to feel, and to be. Parents and teachers can assist the examiner in discussing these aspects of behavior not usually apparent in the typical examination.

Impulsiveness

To the socialized adult the natural child is impulsive and tends to behave without thinking, often unintentionally getting himself into some sort of difficulty. They are "now" oriented children and often react to the environment relative to what is happening at the moment without regard for consequences. They can recognize and discuss consequences one minute, and the next they behave as if the discussion had not occurred. This tendency is not a disorder or neurological problem, but one of difference in thought orientation and process.

Mood Changes

The naturalistic child, because of his lack of attention to

consequences, often reacts emotionally to a situation. He may become angered easily or be exceptionally happy and in a few moments he has switched moods seeming to forget that moments before his world was quite different. Because these children are so intense and involved in their world of spatial and fantasy orientation, they are vulnerable to the whims of the environment. They have difficulty modulating their behavior because they are not language oriented.

High Interest in Visual Stimuli

Many naturalistic children are addicted television watchers. Television offers a visual world far more stimulating than their surroundings and reaching nearly to the realm of their own rich fantasy world. Cartoons, science fiction, and vivid visual programs provide for them a highly motivating and satisfying world. They may miss the important meanings of their experiences and only retain the nature of the experience without evaluation.

Egocentric Behavior

Since the naturalistic child engages in a personal world of fantasy and nonverbal behavior, he may be very egocentric and see the world only in terms of his own response to it. He has a tendency to want to persist in his own pursuits without regard for convention or authority. Thus, this child needs much attention in values and language orientation.

Language Sequential Organization Difficulties

The naturalistic child often has difficulties in recalling directionally oriented words and phrases. For example, if asked what day comes before Tuesday, he may say Wednesday; for the month coming after June he may say May. He may have difficulty recalling the correct sequence of the seasons but be able to report all of them. Often such children give east as the direction of the setting sun and if questioned are uncertain if it is east or west though they know it is one of them. This confusion may be based in the difficulty of translating verbal representations into spatial directions because of the right hemispheric tendency to work from right to left. The child learns that his natural hunch is wrong and often attempts to think of the opposite direction from what he usually "feels." But his mental manipulation can be difficult and consequently he forgets which one is the natural hunch and which is the actual direction.

Disorganization in General Behavior at Home and School

Often the parents and teachers will see a general disorganization in behavior at home and school. The natural child may attempt to go in two directions at once and constantly forget where he put something. His room is often a shambles and attempts to organize him are often futile. His desk at school may be stuffed with so many paper and personal items that he can never find his pencil. He may even forget that he was looking for his pencil. Many children are disorganized, however, and it is only when this trait is observed in the context of several others that it may be indicative of a naturalized thought process.

Interest in Animals

Often the naturalistic child has a strong interest in animals though he may have difficulty, due to disorganization, in being a good caretaker. They appear to relate well to animals, and this is likely related to their strong orientation to nonverbal behavior which makes them highly sensitive to the needs of animals.

The Class Clown

There are many reasons why children may become the class

clown, and naturalistic orientation is a strong possibility. The naturalistic child enjoys sounds, facial expressions, and non-verbal communication. For this reason they often make good clowns, making all sorts of strange noises, faces, and indulging in other forms of mimicry to gain attention and admiration from others.

Summary

The foregoing clinical signs include thirty-two possible indicators of potential naturalistic behavior characteristics in the Alpha child. The list is certainly not exhaustive and the examiner must use his professional judgement in attempting to formulate a potential syndrome of naturalistic behavioral patterns. Certainly, it can be recognized that many of these indicators are also those associated with learning disabilities, emotional or social disturbance, and a host of other typical learning or behavioral disorders. While a child who has some sort of disorder may exhibit many of these factors, many children who are thought to have a disorder may well be Alpha children. In the former case we may find pathological signs in a child, but in the latter we may find not pathology but simply difference which must be dealt with through educational techniques rather than clinical therapy. The decision is not easy for the psychologist but certainly this viewpoint can significantly alter our approach to a child's problems. If we see him as "sick," our response will be quite different than if we see a child who simply has not learned appropriate social behavior due to a difference in developmental and neurological organization.

Classroom Observation of Naturalistic Tendencies

The teacher, working with the psychologist, can assist greatly in observation of many of the foregoing clinical factors. But she also needs guidelines for an extensive system of observing behavior in the classroom which may assist in identification of the naturalistic child. The following lists of behavior are designed to closely follow the right and left hemispheric tendencies outlined earlier in the book. The two lists cited in the first chapter were those most often appearing in the literature. For purposes of the classroom teacher, the following list was developed so that an equalized and correlated list could be used in the classroom. The list is somewhat arbitrarily developed and, as such, does not fit the general model exactly. But it should serve to provide a general orientation for observation and discussion by the teacher, psychologist, and parents.

Left Minded Characteristics		*Right Minded Characteristics*	
A1	VE-Verbally expressive	A2	ME-Motorically expressive
B1	L-Logical	B2	I-Intuitive
C1	OS-Orderly and sequential	C2	HG-Holistic and gestalt
D1	T-Time orientation	D2	S-Spatial orientation
E1	SV-Socialized values	E2	NV-Naturalistic values
F1	AA-Aggressive assertive	F2	SA-Submissive accepting
G1	AT-Abstract thought	G2	CT-Concrete thought
H1	VT-Vertical thought-structured	H2	LT-Lateral thought-creative
I1	O-Objective	I2	S-Subjective
J1	CM-Conventional motor organization	J2	Mixed and unconventional motor organization

These ten socialized and naturalized behavioral, cognitive, affective, and personality factors display characteristics which can be designed to provide a structured means of objectively scoring socialized-naturalized factors in the classroom. It may provide a somewhat artificial structure based as much upon theory as fact. But, when used by the teacher and psychologist, it will force us to look in a new way at behavior. That process will hopefully give us additional insights into the behavior of children. The two lists of behaviors can also be thought of as the socialized and naturalized mode of thinking or perceptual orientation. In the so-called "average" child we would expect a general correlation between the two modes of thought demonstrating that while one or the other mode may be the dominant mode of thought for the child, he is able to modulate between the two, displaying nearly equal competence in both. The children with whom we should be concerned are those who have much higher scores in one or the other mode. Our concern here is for the naturalistic child but we have already mentioned

Factor	Socialized mode	

A1   *Verbal expressive*   0-1-2-3-4
1. Displays appropriate vocabulary for age. — — — — —
2. Speaks with good syntax and language structure. — — — — —
3. Answers specific questions adequately. — — — — —
4. Describes personal thoughts in proper sequence. — — — — —
5. Asks questions in order to obtain information. — — — — —

B1   *Logical*
1. Shows objectivity in attitude towards others. — — — — —
2. Evaluates situations and personal behavior. — — — — —
3. Recognizes consequences of personal behavior. — — — — —
4. Selects appropriate goals and personal behavior. — — — — —
5. Understands reasons for rules. — — — — —

C1   *Orderly and sequential*
1. Recalls a series of directions. — — — — —
2. Follows a series of directions. — — — — —
3. Displays appropriate personal organization. — — — — —
4. Displays sequential pattern of thought. — — — — —
5. Predicts outcomes of behavior. — — — — —

D1   *Time orientation*
1. Knows sequence of days, weeks, months, or time of day. — — — — —
2. Understands and uses numbers appropriate for age. — — — — —
3. Aware of and adheres to time-related activities. — — — — —
4. Paces personal activity to time limits. — — — — —
5. Uses time to organize self. — — — — —

E1   *Socialized values*
1. Recognizes and uses appropriate social behaviors. — — — — —
2. Understands situational rules of right and wrong. — — — — —
3. Displays appropriate remorse or guilt for misbehavior. — — — — —
4. Strives for social acceptance. — — — — —
5. Has socially appropriate and acceptable goals. — — — — —

F1   *Aggressive and assertive*
1. Is personally assertive with others. — — — — —
2. Has a desire to compete. — — — — —
3. Concerned about fair play and cooperative activity. — — — — —
4. Appears to want rules in games and work. — — — — —
5. Shows personal motivation to achieve. — — — — —

G1   *Abstract thought*
1. Can discuss relationships in abstract terms. — — — — —
2. Can apply rules to abstract situations. — — — — —
3. Enjoys mathematical games and tasks. — — — — —
4. Can discuss remote relationships. — — — — —
5. Displays logical problem-solving ability. — — — — —

H1   *Vertical thought - structured*
1. Can apply rules to problems in math. — — — — —
2. Can predict outcomes in familiar situations. — — — — —
3. Displays deductive ability. — — — — —
4. Is able to classify and categorize information. — — — — —
5. Displays understanding of social behavior consequences. — — — — —

I1   *Objective*
1. Can use criterion to evaluate situations or information. — — — — —
2. Learns and uses social rules. — — — — —
3. Displays a lack of bias in appropriate situations. — — — — —
4. Can remove self from situation and evaluate. — — — — —
5. Can listen and accept viewpoints of others. — — — — —

J1   *Conventional motor organization*
1. Organizes work appropriately from left to right. — — — — —
2. Uses right-handed mode of writing. — — — — —
3. Able to read or sequence left to right without difficulty. — — — — —
4. Organizes work well on paper with proper spacing and size. — — — — —
5. Has good balance and coordination. — — — — —

                       Subtotal — — — — —
                            Total _____

Figure 6:

Factor	Naturalized Mode	
A2	*Motorically expressive*	0-1-2-3-4

A2	*Motorically expressive*

0-1-2-3-4

A2 *Motorically expressive* 0-1-2-3-4
1. Enjoys physical activities and games. - - - - -
2. Likes to draw, paint, build and make things. - - - - -
3. Relates to others physically; touching; hitting. - - - - -
4. Talks with many gestures and physical movements. - - - - -
5. Displays general restlessness during verbal or highly structured situations. - - - - -

B2 *Intuitive*
1. Exhibits high sensitivity to the feelings of others. - - - - -
2. Displays frequent mood changes, appears introspective, daydreams, and gains insight about others. - - - - -
3. Sees the practical basis of a problem. - - - - -
4. Highly responsive to music and situational mood. - - - - -
5. Highly aware of sensory information in the environment. (tastes, smells, colors, sounds, touch) - - - - -

C2 *Holistic and gestalt*
1. Sees higher purpose or general goals but may miss specific goals or sequence of behavior. - - - - -
2. Attempts to understand complex situations in a general way without regard for details. - - - - -
3. Perceives whole of words, phrases and sentences. - - - - -
4. Has general feeling about pictures or objects but can remember few details. - - - - -
5. Remembers visual aspects of people and objects but forgets names. - - - - -

D2 *Spatial orientation*
1. Highly sophisticated visual memory, knows and describes past events but cannot remember dates, time, or names. - - - - -
2. Has excellent movement capacity in activities. - - - - -
3. Orients to either right or left without defined preference or outside supervision. - - - - -
4. Poor directional orientation but good memory for physical characteristics of past locations. - - - - -
5. Enjoys open spaces and lack of crowding. - - - - -

E2 *Naturalistic values*
1. Uses situational values rather than cultural norms. - - - - -
2. Considers experiences of value if they are self-stimulating. - - - - -
3. Has a need for immediate gratification. - - - - -
4. Tends to see self as important and as the center of all things. Feels a oneness with all. - - - - -
5. Displays shifting friendships, on-off depending on personal moods at the time. - - - - -

F2 *Submissive and accepting*
1. Tends to be accepting of others without personal commitment to them, autonomous. - - - - -
2. Tends to accept aggression without a need to counter. - - - - -
3. Submits to compromise rather than conflict. - - - - -
4. Changes goals if extensive blocking occurs. - - - - -
5. Becomes aggressive when others try to direct him but will submit if he simply has to stop activity. - - - - -

G2 *Concrete thought*
1. Displays apparent high degree of "common sense." - - - - -
2. Tends to state things as they are. - - - - -
3. Tends to need sensory input with information. - - - - -
4. Not socially astute. - - - - -
5. Has difficulty seeing remote relationships. - - - - -

H2 *Lateral thought - creative*
1. Tends to be imaginative and fantasy oriented. - - - - -
2. Develops unusual responses and solutions. - - - - -
3. Tends to develop a variety of thoughts surrounding one stimulus. - - - - -
4. Tends to automatically elaborate on ideas. - - - - -
5. Can visualize and create unusual "things." - - - - -

I2	*Subjective*	0-1-2-3-4
	1. Relates goals of group to self.	- - - - -
	2. Evaluates others on the basis of personal beliefs.	- - - - -
	3. Embues objects and others with personal characteristics.	- - - - -
	4. Often responds in a highly emotional way to situations of stress or conflict.	- - - - -
	5. Determined to believe personal values and constructs.	- - - - -
J2	*Mixed and unconventional motor organization*	
	1. Has tendency to reverse letters or the order of letters.	- - - - -
	2. Has a tendency to use a different hand for various tasks.	- - - - -
	3. Displays visual-motor difficulty in fine motor tasks that are educationally structured but not in personal activity.	- - - - -
	4. Has a tendency to reverse spoken words in syntax or in writing.	- - - - -
	5. Poor organization skills or written work and in general behavior.	- - - - -

Subtotal - - - - -

Total _____

that the socialized (Theta) child without adequate naturalized abilities may also have much difficulty in learning or behavioral adjustment.

The checklists of specific behavior (Figure 6) for each one of the characteristics given above can be scored by using the class as a norm group. Five levels of scoring are suggested, 0 for inadequate, 1 for minimum ability, 2 for average, 3 for slightly better than average ability, and 4 for superior ability. The class group is used as the norm and each child is compared to the class as a whole to determine the score. The average child should score a total of 200, or 100 for Socialized Mode and 100 for the Naturalized Mode. This system of scoring is not intended to be a sophisticated statistical computation but rather a practical means of giving the teacher some method of comparing children in her classroom.

REFERENCES

1. W. Ferinden, Jr. and S. Jackson: *Educational Interpretation of the Wechsler Intelligence Scale for Children.* Linden, NJ, Remediation Associates, 1969.
2. H. Yahraes: *Detection and Prevention of Learning Disorders.* Rockville, Md, National Institute of Mental Health, 1976.

Chapter 7

THE ALPHA CHILD AND READING

WHEN children learn to read, we as educators and parents like to feel that we taught them to read. Idealistically, learning to read is a process of personal initiative and directed experience in which both the teacher and learner play an active role. It is so for many of the children who come to school to learn, but Alpha children come to school for many reasons, not the least of which is because "that is where the action is" and because there is no where else one is allowed to go when one is only five or six years of age. So it begins, this experience that may never end.

Reading is not just a skill: it is a tool whereby worlds are opened to the child that could not exist without words printed in neat and orderly fashion on a page. Most children learn because they want to and because it is expected of them. The Alpha child may not learn for the conventional reasons, nor will he learn in the conventional way unless we know *how* he learns. Our study of the Alpha child and how he learns has opened the door to knowledge that is important not only to the Alpha child but to all children. Before we enter this unusual world let us state, for our purposes here, why we feel children should learn to read.

1. Words convey history and history establishes our place in time, our meaning as a culture, our heritage, and future. Words bring the past and the future into full view when neither can exist without language and words. More importantly, language symbols, verbal and nonverbal, provide the means of communicating information and ideas. Upon such ideas our minds can grow into expanded awareness and being.
2. Words provide an abstract way of learning about the feelings of others, of their hopes, ideas, and concerns.
3. Words provide the means of filing, in retrievable form, our

own past experience and future dreams. Language and words define our own history, our personal place in time and place.

4. Words provide an extensive data bank of information that can be used to evaluate, to elaborate, to synthesize, and to create new information and ideas.
5. Words provide the mechanical means to travel from practical to abstract and back again to practical.
6. Words provide the means to test the environment surrounding us, to learn of its nature, to find ways to live in harmony with the world about us.
7. Words and books provide the means of giving each of us independence in personal growth for we can seek out information that is important to us as individuals. Words bring the thoughts and knowledge of great teachers and philosophers to us as if the person were there.
8. Words and books open the storehouses of knowledge to us all.
9. Words bring the potential for personal meaning.

It seems important to list these few goals for learning to read words in addition to recognizing the task of learning a language since it is obvious that these goals could not be accomplished for each child simply by learning to talk. Further, too often the goals of the school relative to reading programs appear to state somewhat different values relative to learning to read. Below are listed some of the implied goals of reading in school. They are not as unrealistic as they may first appear.

1. One learns to read to become literate.
2. One learns to read because that is what one goes to school for.
3. One learns to read in order to obtain a passing grade so one can pass to the next grade to learn to read better.
4. One learns to read because it is fun to read.
5. One learns to read because parents expect one to and because personal worth is determined by how well one reads.
6. One learns to read because learning is the work of children.
7. One learns to read so that one can become a productive

spatial cognition, are integrated in order to recognize and comprehend written words. In primitive societies, language developed over long periods of time prior to the use of written symbols to represent the spoken language. Written language, as a major means for communication, has been a rather late development in civilized cultures. The first writing most likely was a pictorial representation of language, a somewhat direct representation in pictures of what sounds usually conveyed, hence, the many linguistic-spatial symbols of ancient cultures in which pictorial representations were placed in some sequence to convey a thought or action. The hand signs of the deaf and the language of ancient Indian tribes both represent not only language symbols through movement but more specifically a means of conveying past and future thought in the form of movements. This is a highly right hemispheric process of communication because it is a form of communication without verbal expression. It may be safe to assume that this primitive communication demonstrates again an earlier discussion. It was pointed out that the earliest learning of the child is nonverbal and sensory centered in the right hemisphere. It is also suggested that the earliest thought processes in man were also more sensory based and right hemispheric. Sounds and sensory information of movement, touch, smell, taste, and vision were all used by early man to communicate prior to the establishment of complex speech sounds which came to represent and supplement the many sensory-spatial movements. Not until a complex linguistic oral language was developed did written symbols come to represent more and more precisely language sounds. Thus, both in young children and in ancient cultures, we see a similarity in developmental growth from right hemispheric perception and communication to more linguistic or language based communication. Developmentally, the child first learns the spatial and sensory elements of his environment. He sees, feels, tastes, moves, and hears his world. He perceives color, depth, form, direction, texture, taste, size and weight, smell, and behavior in his world about him. This is a right hemispheric process with some minimal auditory components. As this information grows he learns to associate simple sounds and finally to attach words to perceptual data. Moving objects cause sound and the sound comes to predict the existence of moving objects. The movement of objects comes to be called "rattle," "roll," "bounce," or simply "move." A child learns to sit in a chair before he learns to call it a chair. He recognizes the word sit and chair before he is able to say sit or chair. He first learns to listen to sounds and associate them with all of the perceptual information he has learned. As his store of auditory data grows he practices. "Ma-Ma," mother smiles, he says it again, "Ma-Ma," and Ma-Ma comes to represent his mother. He touches, tastes, feels, watches, and eventually listens. After listening, testing, practicing and feedback from Ma-Ma, he then is assured that the speech sounds "Ma-Ma" represents mother. He is learning the language system. Sounds come to represent reality.

Deprive the child of adequate perceptual experiences and he has no basis for language. Deprive him of language experience and feedback following perceptual experiences and he does not learn to talk. Deprive him of learning to speak and his learning world is greatly constricted for he cannot represent reality with words, he cannot "think" abstractly. Abstraction implies that we are using some sort of symbol system to represent an object, an action, or an experience. A child eats an apple, he tastes it, sees it, and feels it. He knows about apples. Give him the sounds for the word apple and teach him that these sounds "represent" the apple, and he can "talk" about apples. He remembers how an apple looks, tastes, smells, and feels, and he understands the word "apple" in relation to the sensory data that is recalled. Deprive him of the sensory experience with apples and the word has no meaning for he cannot abstract something in language in the early stages of learning unless he has had *experience* with the abstractions. The left hemisphere and language provide the computer system for storing, classifying, categorizing, and symbolizing information about the real world. Sensory experience provides the basis for using language and language provides an orderly way to recreate, to recall experience in order to learn more experience.

For the teacher the key neurological words are abstraction or representation, sensory data, and imagery. Sensory data is accumulated first and is most basic to all learning. Language occurs with experience and helps to abstract that experience. Language representation frequently elicits images which more directly represent reality in an abstract form. Both left and right hemispheric functions are required in language and communication when using words as opposed to pictorial units. But then, we complicate the process: we introduce written words.

Written words provide a visual representation of sounds which provide an auditory representation of imagery. This provides a sensory re-experience of reality. Visual-spatial representations or written words, to auditory representations, or sounds, and back to visual spatial imagery representing the actual object or experience, then, comprehension and understanding. This is the simple process of reading. But it is not so simple is it? All of this we hope to teach through learning sounds and recognizing written symbols. How many teachers truly understand the complexity of what they are attempting to "teach" a child? If they did they would most likely not begin at all. Several problems can make it difficult or impossible for the child to learn to read:

1. a lack of adequate perceptual experience
2. a lack of language experience
3. poor feedback during critical periods of learning language
4. difficulties in motoric and directional orientation
5. inability to coordinate language and spatial information
6. difficulty in production of speech sounds
7. difficulties in classification and association between auditory and spatial images
8. inability to recall imagery and produce it
9. inability to differentiate forms and spatial cues
10. difficulties in auditory discrimination
11. inability to use proper syntax
12. emotional and social deprivation inhibiting expression

These are but a few of the many problems which may interfere with the process of spatial-language development. Language and reading are interneurosensory processes; they require the integration of both hemispheres. Our concern here is the discussion of how the naturalistic child has difficulty in this process. But before we turn our attention to the Alpha child, we should state the learning sequence of reading in its most logical form:

1. perceptual experience
2. auditory experience and the development of inner language
3. listening to speech sounds and associating them to experience
4. producing and practicing sounds and words
5. recognizing sounds and words in written form
6. producing written forms of words

In summary, the process includes experience, listening, talking, reading, and writing. Our most recent experiences in schools suggest that the following are indicative of how poor reading instruction can occur:

1. We attempt to teach children to read who may have little or no verbal experience with the words they must read.
2. We often use spoken words for which the children may have no perceptual experience.
3. We teach children to read words which cannot be represented in imagery in the child's experience.
4. AND, we teach children to write words which they cannot say and have no experience from which to produce imagery.

Most recently we have added insult to children by suggesting that if they cannot learn to read then it is their fault because the central nervous system has a problem. We call it "dyslexia" and produce many methods of attempting to solve a problem which lies not so much with the child as with our incomplete understanding of how he learns. In over eight hundred cases of children with learning disabilities and reading disorders we have seen less than ten in a clinical setting who could be called dyslexic. The remainder of the children had difficulties in the developmental process and, most importantly, there were gross inaccuracies in the way they were being taught to read relative to their developmental and neurological styles of perception. What has occurred is that we have lumped all developmental difficulties into one great educational delusion called "dyslexia." And there stands the Alpha child, smiling, and holding a great key to our whole dilemma, for in his peculiar learning style we may discover why many children do not learn to read.

In the first place, dyslexia is not a "condition." It is not a single disorder which can be classified simply as a difficulty in learning to read. Our own definition of "dyslexia" includes only those children who demonstrate a complete and remarkable inability to translate spatial imagery into auditory or language imagery or vice versa. That elminates the dozens of poor children paraded in front of us who could read but were having many problems. It includes only those who cannot learn to read because, in fact, the neurological potential for the process is lacking. The remainder of the children are children with a variety of learning problems — and our smiling Alpha child.

The naturalized child loves images but not words. When the naturalized child looks at a word he may tend to look at it in the same way he looks at a picture, with a series of eye movements designed to catch the most important aspect of the word in order to translate it wholly into imagery meaning as quickly as possible. This "gestalt" tendency is the right hemisphere's method of perception. There is no particular logic sequence, or rationale used. The child attempts to perceive "whole" meaning. This is truly what is meant by a "visual" learning child. Reading specialists have long been aware that certain children learn best by the "visual" method. In the Mills reading test[1] the child is tested to determine which of several modalities, including both auditory and visual, he is best able to use for learning. The Mills test is one of the few existing means of testing children in this manner. The psychologist can determine this modality preference through the usual word recognition tests when a child attempts to guess or say the whole word as has been mentioned in preceding discussions. While many children who have not developed adequate word recognition skills may also do this, with the naturalized child we also look for many of the other indicators cited earlier. In the past, however, reading specialists have never attempted to understand why certain children were "visual" learners. Now we know why at least many children approach reading in this manner and, with the additional theory cited here about the naturalistic child, we can now see that the visual learner may also be a child who learns to perceive not only words in this manner but other information as well.

The tendency to utilize many visual cues in order to grasp the "gestalt meaning" of a word may include the use of configuration, general structure, certain key letters, or context. The Alpha child prefers this method rather than the phonetic, structural analysis which is a left hemisphere method of word recognition. The naturalized child learns to read faster and more efficiently through "sight" approaches. However, in recent years objections to the "look and say" approach have made the sight reading technique not only unacceptable but "old-fashioned," and a host of educational biases have developed so that most teachers are strongly against such an approach. Yet, the naturalized child learns best through this approach.

One of the most fascinating "fads" in recent educational development has been the use of the so-called "VAKT" approach for problem readers and, particularly, for the dyslexic reader. This method combines all the sense modalities, visual, auditory, tactile, and kinesthetic, in an attempt to give the child the greatest opportunity to learn.

If a child today has difficulty in learning to read by the conventional phonetic or linguistic approaches, he is often exposed to the VAKT approach as the means to "correct" his problem. Unfortunately, the VAKT approach is usually used to learn phonetic structural analysis of words, exactly what the naturalized child cannot do. Since the naturalized child frequently has directional and sequential difficulties in motor organization, he becomes even more confused when all of the modalities such as visual, auditory, tactile, and kinesthetic processes are combined. These are VISUAL learners and the combination of several modalities may confuse the child even more. Thus, the VAKT approach, while appropriate for children with certain perceptual and auditory disorders, is a disaster for the naturalized child. But an interesting phenomenon has been noted in our clinic with naturalized children who have been exposed to a highly phonetic or VAKT approach from the outset of reading instruction in first grade. They are taught that when one reads, one uses a phonetic approach. These children believe that this is so and attempt to learn this way, establishing habit patterns in reading, ineffective as they are, which are phonetic in nature. Thus, they may attempt to sound out each word with little retention and continuing confusion. Because they have been taught that this is the way to read, they persist. Even when they are exposed to whole word approaches, the means by which they learn most efficiently, they do poorly initially because of the phonetic conditioning. In essence, the early phonetic conditioning renders their natural approach useless. Fortunately, with some reconditioning, they quickly begin to develop whole word approaches.

We will discuss shortly a variety of approaches in reading for these children but first an important point must be made which should restore dignity and meaning to the structural analysis reading specialist. While the naturalistic child will learn more easily through the whole word approach, he should also be given phonetic instruction as an encouragement toward the language orientation. He may always cling to his naturalistic mode of learning and behavior, but we need to always attempt to stimulate his deficit modality, language, in an attempt to force development in both areas of functioning. Thus, while we recognize his preferred modality and teach the whole word approach to the child, we also introduce and use phonetic analysis as a supportive approach to that method. The use of both approaches does not seem to confuse children taught in this manner and actually is not so difficult when we recognize that the language child learns phonetic approaches and supports them with some whole word perception. For the naturalistic child the process is simply reversed.

Phonetic analysis forces the child to learn sequence, specificity in association, logic, and integration. The phonetic approach, aside from the additional assistance it may give the child, performs a training function of neurological process. For this reason, the naturalistic child needs both whole word and phonetic approaches. The process involves, first, learning the whole word and then word parts, blends, vowels, and basic units, rather than beginning with the units and proceeding to whole words. All the "left minded" teacher has to do is think "backwards," remembering that the Alpha child has had to do it all of his life.

As we discuss some possible approaches in reading skill development for the naturalistic child, it should be kept in mind that though it will be assumed that the teacher is working with a child who truly exhibits such a syndrome, few children in actual practice will exhibit the total syndrome. Most children seen clinically will be children who are strongly oriented toward naturalistic tendencies, but who also have available socialized capabilities. Much of the approach in whole word strategies can be used as supplementary material for many children. The following list of difficulties will often be seen when the naturalistic child begins to learn reading skills.

1. A tendency to have difficulty with syntax aside from problems in word attack skills. Language development activities in verbal expressions should also be strengthened. Some of the suggested approaches will assist in this difficulty but the teacher should continuously strive to strengthen language expressive skills. This will be particularly true with older children in later elementary or secondary levels.
2. A tendency to "guess" the word rather than to use various sight and phonetic skills to actually perceive the word as it is.
3. A tendency to word call without developing comprehensive imagery in association with the word. Care should be taken not to allow a child to simply learn to recognize a word without understanding the meaning of the word.
4. A tendency to visually sight the word from right to left rather than to scan the word in left to right sequence.
5. A tendency to become confused when both writing and recognition skills are combined. More about writing will be discussed in Chapter 8.

The following approaches are given to be integrated into the particular style or approach selected by the teacher with the child. The following list of approaches comprise a range of possible techniques.

GENERAL PRINCIPLES USED IN
THE WHOLE WORD APPROACH

Language Experience Approaches Can Be Used Both to Introduce New Words and to Build Upon the Child's Existing Vocabulary

The language experience approach used here suggests having the child express himself through a variety of means in his own vocabulary, and this vocabulary is then used to structure short stories or sentences which the child learns to read. An approach based on instant whole word recognition requires repetition, general structural analysis, breaking the words into basic parts or word roots, and studying prefixes and suffixes and/or syllables. The stories or sentences are either written on the board while the child tells the teacher his thoughts, or his story is tape recorded and later typed for the child to read individually with the teacher or tutor. The following possible approaches may be used in this process:

a. Explain to the child that he is to tell of something that happened to him over the weekend, on vacation, or of an interesting event that has occurred in his life.
b. Give the child definite subjects and verbs and ask him to make a sentence using these words. In this manner nouns and verbs can be introduced early in a more formal fashion and combined with linguistic approaches such as rhyming words, word groups, or prefix-suffix groups.
c. Ask more than one child to participate with the teacher in making up a story, which is then typed for the entire group.
d. Teach the child that stories should contain an introduction, a description of characters, the development of a situation or event, and a conclusion. The child is asked to make up his own story, or the teacher gives him a basic outline of characters and situations which he then elaborates into a story.

The use of the tape recorder, while initially inhibiting, often becomes quite stimulating to the child and their stories become more and more elaborate. These are placed in each child's own story book which he then rereads from time to time, reinforcing the words which he has learned. Repetition is the key and the child should reread the story until he is able to read each story without any errors. Words which are consistently missed are given again and again in future stories.

One aspect of today's reading programs, particularly the individualized programs, which we have noted is that many children appear to proceed through the program with increasing reading skill but often display what we call "pseudo reading competency." Our work has not allowed an investigation into this phenomenon at this point but we would encourage educators to consider such research. Our concept is as follows. Children are guided through specific small steps in reading growth through individualized techniques and they are able to master each level at least in a marginal way. Their mastery, while in many cases only minimal, does allow them to proceed through the program. But an important element missing, unless the teacher programs for it, is that the child does not use the developed skills in a variety of ways nor are the skills sufficient to insure long-term memory and skill. Thus, as the child proceeds forward he is able to master each level, but many of the specific skills appear to deteriorate during later elementary years. Many specific elements of phonetic and word recognition skills deteriorate to the point that the child reads poorly and with inadequate comprehension. Further, this approach may not provide the child with the interest and endurance to read the longer books and articles required in later school years.

It may well be that many schools have developed programs diversified enough to give children the additional skill of long-term retention. Since we have not researched this phenomenon, its full implication is still unknown, but the evidence of it may exist in declining national test scores for reading and comprehension.

Initial Letter Production and Recognition

The naturalistic child may have difficulty in reversals of letters both in reading and writing. Initial learning of letters should be complete with a multisensory competency.

There is some difficulty with introducing recognition and letter production to naturalistic children, since many of these children will have some directional problems which may confuse them both in production and recognition. If the child is a motorically right hemisphere child, his tendency will be to have difficulty in recognizing letters that have traditionally created problems such as the "b-d," "p-q," or words such as "on-no" and "was-saw." This problem is created due to the child's tendency to want to motorically organize from right to left both in visual recognition and in fine motor reproduction of symbols. This problem certainly creates difficulty in a phonetic approach but it can also pose problems in a structural configuration or whole word approach.

General Configuration Cues

Naturalistic children have a tendency to recognize symbols and words with a total and holistic perception. The following configuration illustrates the technique of gross analysis.

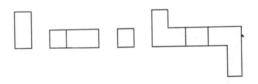

While socialized and phonetically oriented individuals have great difficulty in "reading" the configuration, individuals who have a tendency toward spatial perception can often read with ease, "I am a boy." This has been demonstrated with many adults, including teachers, and it is always interesting to find that there is a great variation in ability to read this phrase. We have found that this is a good example of how an individual may attempt to perceive not only a word but an entire phrase in a holistic manner. Once a child begins to use such an approach many other phrases can be "guessed" with increasing accuracy. In the more conventional style, configuration usually involves drawing around the edges of words to illustrate specific configuration, in the following manner.

This approach, when used with other whole word practice, provides an additional cue for the child. Obviously, the latter approach is limited in that so many words have similar configuration but quite different letter structure such as "was-saw," "run-ran," and "see-sun." Yet, when the configuration is combined with specific letter analysis the two cues can assist the child greatly. Further, many of these initial recognition words are ones that will be seen by the child frequently. If the child learns, through repetition or drill, that the words "ran" and "run" are both words which require the "r" sound in the beginning and the "n" sound in the ending, then the change in the middle letter can be learned. Configuration will not assist the child tremendously except to cue him that here is one of those words which is either "run" or "ran." The phonetic elements here may be introduced along with general whole word recognition and configuration.

Configuration, usually, is only a supplementary approach in learning to read and with the naturalistic child it remains much the same. But the naturalistic child will depend much more on configuration as part of a total perceptual process than most children. Many commercial educational materials companies have configuration cards which consist of an entire set of configuration practice materials. The teacher is encouraged to investigate this approach in more detail using such materials. It should also be remembered that we encourage a sight approach with phonetic or linguistic reinforcement.

Basic Rhythmic Words

Naturalistic children do tend to read words spatially, and they are also often children who love music and rhythm. Music and rhythm, particularly singing, are not often used in introducing words to children in any reading approach. Singing and rhythm make reading much easier and meaningful for many children, in addition to aiding the stutterer in speaking more fluently. There is an interesting phenomenon which occurs in many children who stutter which is not generally known by teachers. While the basis for stuttering may range from emotional difficulties to actual neurological dysfunction in speech and articulation, it has been observed that many stuttering children can sing without stuttering. Language production is primarily a left hemisphere function, while rhythm and certain aspects of musical ability are often more related to right hemisphere function. It may be that by combining the elements of both language and rhythm the right or nonlanguage hemisphere provides more reinforcement for the language hemisphere allowing the child to overcome the stuttering. It should be noted here that while we refer to the right hemisphere as the nonlanguage hemisphere this is not always the case. In some children the combination is reversed with the left hemisphere assuming spatial capacities and the right assuming language. It does not interfere with our theory here except that it would be more appropriate to say "the opposite hemisphere." Since, however, in most cases the lateralization of function is in the stated hemispheres, we will use the right for spatial and the left for language.

We are not concerned here with the stuttering child but with the possibility that, for many children who have sequential language problems, a singing and rhythm approach may assist in the general whole word concept. Toward this end the following activities are suggested.

a. Small groups of children may be given practice each day by singing specific songs in which they must read the words, including many of the elementary and introductory words. Often children can remember songs but not what they have read. Think of the children who learn to read commercial words on television but do not read well. A creative teacher can even have the children write and sing their own original songs to the music of more familiar songs.

b. Children can have group choral reading exercises each day in which lists of basic rhyming words such as "pan," "tan," "ran," and so forth can be read with some rhythm. Children love nonsense and vivid phrases which they can read over and over. The Sullivan Reading Series[2] uses this approach as a regular reading recognition process, though the phrases are neither read in unison nor are they usually nonsense. For example, "A Tan Dog Sits In a Pan." A group of such phrases could be printed by the children on cards and read each day, as an exercise, by the entire group as the teacher selects different ones in a varying order. The addition of music to such practice adds greatly to the fun the children have.

c. The process above can also be used in prefix-suffix practice so that the children learn all of the usual prefix-suffix combinations without words. Many children learn their alphabet initially as the "A-B-C" song, and we find many adults who still use this elementary song to remember the alphabet even if they do not freely admit it. Songs and rhythm games could be used to learn prefix-suffix combinations. With this introduction the classroom teacher should be able to think of many additional possibilities.

Basic Sight Vocabulary

A basic sight vocabulary should be developed and maintained through a variety of techniques. Most teachers are familiar with the basic Dolch Sight vocabulary words. Too often the sight vocabulary is introduced as a series of "to be learned" words with little imagination and elaboration. Just as the phonetic approach is the key to decoding for the socialized or right hemispheric youngster, so the sight vocabulary is the key to decoding for the naturalistic right hemispheric child. A phonetic approach is more logical in learning to read for if the child can merely master the basic rules he will be able to decode an endless number of words. However, reading is a means of visually decoding words which are part of one's experience, and decoding words for which experience does not exist is less than helpful. The first problem for the naturalistic child and eventually the Alpha adult is to learn to speak of one's feelings, to find verbal expression for all of the sensitivity and awareness that runs rampant through the mind. The basic sight vocabulary is a simple beginning, a place to first tell of what one feels inside. The naturalistic child has much to tell and the sequential and complex world of phonetic sounds appears too mechanical and restricting to express all that is felt. Thus, it must always be remembered that the Alpha child is often filled with much more imagination and dreams than can be easily told. Our task is to first give the child practice in speaking, in learning to describe what is known and felt inside.

If the naturalistic child cannot learn words to express himself early, he may cease to learn reading skills and more importantly, he may cease to tell. Just as the child must learn to speak and communicate to express himself, so must he learn to express himself verbally before he can read. His impatience with order and structure often preclude the long hours which phonetic development requires. If he is able to learn initial reading skills quickly then he may be more tolerant of the structure and order represented in phonetic approaches. The basic sight vocabulary can provide the initial holistic and rapid growth the child needs in order to learn enough words to feel some competence and trust in the written word. But it should be remembered that these children require much opportunity to talk, to express in some consistent manner what they feel and know. Following this sort of activity and combined with it the child needs to learn as many basic words for his vocabulary level as early as possible. Using sight vocabularies should provide expression for the child's present experience and serve as a means of subtle introduction of basic words which are not part of his vocabulary. For these reasons, the use of the sight vocabulary should be one in which the words are used in a variety of functional and realistic ways. The following general suggestions will give the teacher some guidelines to enlarge the basic sight vocabulary.

a. The basic sight words should be introduced, as much as

possible, with the language experience approaches mentioned earlier. The teacher should avoid introducing the words merely as sight words to be memorized. The stories and sentences of the child should be elaborated to include as many of the basic sight vocabulary words as possible during each series of language experience activities.

b. As basic words are learned, the child should be encouraged to learn to write the words and make up a series of word cards. These should be laminated and placed in small boxes marked as the parts of speech that they represent such as nouns, verbs, adjectives, and so forth. Very early the teacher should introduce the concepts of parts of speech and assist the child in games or lessons which involve constructing sentences from the word cards by placing them on a blackboard tray or on a table. These sentences can be quite creative and need not make "sense" in the usual concept of a sentence. Rather, they may be very unusual sentences which have meaning and fascination for the child. Sentences made by the child should be typed and filed for future alteration or development. Nearly any sort of sentence is accepted but eventually, as the child develops skills in reading and expression, these sentences may be restructured into more logical and appropriate sentences. The initial sentences are to be enjoyed by the child and given much approval, though the general use of various word parts are always mentioned in passing.

c. Children should be assisted in learning many of the basic stories and sentences of other children when possible. This can be accomplished by having all of the children read in unison other children's stories during specific times each week. The child who is presenting the story may have the other children and the teacher read his story as he presents it on word cards which he has made. If a child likes another child's story and is able to read it, then he may include it in his own reading book which he is structuring.

d. The teacher should present, as regular assignments and as group work, the phonetic sounds and units of words which the children are learning. This should be done only after the child has learned the words within his own story.

e. The children should learn to spell the words in their stories as early as possible utilizing the blackboard frequently for practice and following the approaches in spelling which will be introduced next.

Spelling and Auditory Reinforcement

Children with naturalistic tendencies can often form imagery from auditory stimuli but not directly from visual symbols. Often the naturalistic child has a much higher listening vocabulary than speaking vocabulary. This is generally true of most children and adults. Most of us understand more that we hear and read than we are able to report or explain verbally. There are many reasons for this which are too lengthy for our discussion here, but an essential characteristic is the developmental one mentioned earlier. First, we learn imagery and perceptual images, and then we learn to recognize language associated with the imagery. We are often perplexed when we can recognize something and even know that we know the name but can not remember it. Yet, we easily recognize it when someone else mentions the name. Extensive recall of specific words requires much practice and usage in order to have both efficient recall and expressive abilities. Much of what we learn is only learned at the experience and recognition level. This is also why so many students find it easier to take a multiple choice test than an essay one. The Theta individual is one who can recall and express much verbal content while most of us struggle with an "average" range of receptive and expressive abilities, and the Alpha individual is at the other end of the continuum, recognizing much but unable to recall or express easily. However, this function provides an important reading aide to the naturalistic child as we will see in the following method.

The naturalistic child often remembers a word once it is said to him. Again, this is because he is able to function well at the recognition level but not so well in recall and verbalization. Interestingly enough, if he could find some way of providing auditory input in recognizing words he would tremendously increase his skills in reading. Since he has so much difficulty remembering specific phonetic sounds and integrating them, the phonetic approach is somewhat useless, but if he is asked to say the letters of the word out loud, he will often recognize them. In essence, spelling the words out loud as he looks at them often aides holistic recognition. Thus, one technique which should always be tried is that of having the child say each letter out loud and to see if this assists recall and recognition. It often will.

The foregoing discussion also points out another approach. The child should learn to spell all of the words that he learns to read as he learns to read them. This is not to say that he literally practices each word as he learns it, but lessons in oral spelling should accompany the lessons of sight recognition for each new group of words. He first learns these words auditorily and later learns to write them. The auditory spelling should always precede the actual practice in writing. Learning to spell first and write later is always a good developmental approach, and it is especially helpful to the Alpha child as writing the word prior to learning it may confuse him.

Organizational Skills in Reading

The naturalistic child needs to learn, in a conditioned manner, to scan and look at words from left to right and to organize from left to right. Though it does not receive much emphasis, not all children naturally work or perceive from left to right. Our previous discussions certainly would suggest that this is a problem for the naturalistic child. Activities in spelling, reading, and writing should constantly provide an emphasis on the left to right scanning organization. When letters or words are written on the blackboard they should always be written from left to right. Often the teacher will list a series of words in a vertical fashion down the blackboard. This is easier for the Alpha child, but in as many areas as possible we do not want to always make it "easier" for the Alpha child. Avoiding vertical presentation in favor of listing words and letters from left to right is one area in which the more difficult approach should be taken in order to condition the child to the left/right organization. This approach will also assist him in continually organizing himself and his visual scanning ability in a left to right fashion.

Many times using the finger to follow along under the words as he reads will also assist in both visual coordination and adding sensory input to the notion of working left to right.

Auditory Impress Method

The naturalistic child should be given as much auditory reinforcement of reading as possible. The naturalistic child often does not attend to his own verbalizations as carefully as other children. His sentences may be nonsensical or confused and indicate difficulty in formulating the verbal syntax needed for clear expression. The foregoing discussion about the importance of teaching verbal skills points to this problem. It is important to assist the child in monitoring and altering his own verbal expression in order to state his ideas clearly. Another aide to such a child, as we have mentioned, is that process of hearing words that he is attempting to recognize. A further elaboration of this process is that of giving the child a continuous flow of auditory feedback for his own verbalization. There is a general technique called the "neurological impress" method for children with learning disabilities which involves saying sounds or words directly after the child says them in order to reinforce his sounds and words. While our concern here is not exactly in line with this approach, it is similar in nature. In this case the child reads into a tape recorder and the instructor or another child assists the child in recognizing the correct word. After the child has finished the recording, he then listens to it and reads along with it. He may listen to it several times making sure that he can correct his errors.

This approach is based on the child's need for ego reinforcement. Aside from the pleasure of using his own voice to reinforce his reading, he also gains a more personalized and motivating stimulus from listening to the errors on tape. The child delights in being able to correct himself and he sees real progress. This tape should be saved and the child should review the tape occasionally to assure that retention remains solid. As he makes more tapes for his file, they provide him with a continuing record of his progress throughout the year.

Study Skills and Scanning

The naturalistic child should be taught early the skills involved in searching for information within written paragraphs. Normally, study skills are not important until the child has gained some skill in reading or until reading becomes an act of learning content rather than merely skills. This process should start from the beginning for the naturalistic child. While the naturalistic child will learn to read, his primary mode of getting information from reading in later years will most likely tend toward the scanning. Scanning is sometimes taught as an additional skill to readers, but it becomes a necessity for the Alpha child for he finds conventional reading too slow or laborious. It is also the most natural way for the Alpha child to read. He scans important words or phrases in an article or book and is able to "grasp" the general meaning, concentrating only on parts which are technical or difficult.

Choral Reading

The naturalistic child often finds it easier to learn words if they are combined with a rhythmic pattern. The close tie of right mindedness with rhythm and motoric movement has been mentioned earlier. An approach used in some programs has been that of choral reading which, while it does not provide a major technique, is a supplementary approach. The children practice reading phrases, sentences, or the words of songs and poems through a choral reading exercise. Time is spent not only reading together but also learning intonation and inflection. This process, though sometimes difficult to initiate due to the shyness or inhibitions of the children, can become quite a rewarding experience. Perhaps one of the most common experiences for the adult which demonstrates this phenomenon is that of singing the "Star Spangled Banner" during public events. Many individuals do not know the words alone but find it easy to recall the words when the entire group is singing them. This group reinforcement provides intrinsic satisfaction for both the adult and child which makes it personally motivating.

Memorization

Memorization activity with visual passages provides reinforcement of visual-auditory transfer of imagery. Many a young boy stood in his naturally faded jeans and stammered self-consciously as he recited a morning lesson in front of the class in a one-room school of long ago. Such memorization is nearly unheard of today, for there appears to be no need for it. There are still, however, many older people who fondly remember extensive passages of favorite poems and stories painstakingly learned so long ago. There is little doubt that the purpose of such memorization of poems and short stories had as much to do with the shortage of books and educational materials as it did with simple memory work. But memorization had other rewards more neurologically important if the learning could be accomplished in an atmosphere of acceptance and praise. The process of memorization requires the ability to retain and recall, in sequence, extensive visual imagery. This process is the same as that required to recall whole words. Thus, sensible memory work might still have an important place in the classroom for naturalistic children. The children need not remember entire stories or poems, but some memory work of sentences or phrases might assist as training for the visual retention of words.

The authors have found that many teachers in today's schools no longer are trained in language experience approaches. The foregoing methods can be integrated into a general language experience approach in which specific reading experiences become integrated into a total approach which includes both phonetic and whole word concepts. It is probably true that teaching children through language experience goes beyond the notion of memorizing a list of simple sight words, to require an extensive amount of creative teaching. The basal reading series, the individualized reading approaches, linguistic methods, and the more specialized multisensory approaches all are generally well organized and include extensive teacher guidance manuals which give the teacher structured approaches to follow. While teacher creativity is still required to supplement such materials, too often the approach or method itself becomes the primary organizer for the child. While many teachers would justifiably take exception to the foregoing statement, it must also be recognized that it has a wide-ranging validity in too many classrooms. Further, when compared to the amount of teacher creativity and sensitivity involved in language experience approaches, which by their nature negate extensive standardization, the "series" approaches are much less teacher organized and directed. The teacher, in the "series" approach, becomes more or less a part of the organizational structure of the approach, rather than an organizer of the approach. Due to the deemphasis on sight or whole word approaches in the last twenty years, most teachers in today's schools have either never had exposure to such approaches or they have gladly discarded them.

The loss of the language experience approach has eliminated a valuable and important technique for many children, who, as we have stated, desperately need them. Yet, this is not to say that the newer approaches are not important. It is not and never has been true that all children learn by the same methods. The newer materials in individually guided curricula and commercial materials in various linguistic and phonetic approaches have provided important advances to the theories and application of reading methodology. The field of education has long been afflicted with a tendency to discard the old and incorporate the new without adequate understanding of how children learn. We must state a general educational principle which is as true today as it was twenty years ago. The teaching of reading depends not so much on which methods are used as it does on the skill of the teacher in selecting the appropriate method for each child. More than any other reason, the economics of education has dealt the death blow to many of the older methods of teaching. It is difficult for most school systems to adopt more than one series or set of educational materials. Consequently, most schools select a few materials which must be used "system wide" as a matter of economics. Thus, economics and the need for standardized teaching methods have provided a strong impetus to the adoption and use of "system wide" reading approaches even though there are seldom any classrooms of children who will all learn by the same approach. The language experience requires a much greater teacher effort in the preparation and use of personalized reading materials. It requires that the teacher spend a great deal of time in understanding and adopting methods for each child. It increases the personalization and teacher-pupil interaction time. For these reasons, in the 1960s when classroom enrollment swelled, most teachers were glad to discard the language experience approach in favor of more individualized standardized approaches which require less teacher creativity and student-teacher time. Now, with decreasing enrollments and the realization that the language experience approach has a place with many children, perhaps we can persuade educators to consider once more the approaches outlined here.

Experience Charts

For the child with naturalistic tendencies it is often difficult to verbalize those visual experiences that occurred sometime in the past. Cameras hold many possibilities for these children. The process of choosing a self-selected subject matter and the process of taking the picture gives the youngster something on which to base his oral expression. It is not only personal and meaningful oral expression for the child, but it reveals to the teacher those things which are important to the child. The stories told by the child about his photographs should be placed in a book which he can keep and refer to for practice in reading and for adding information if he chooses. The stories can be told to the teacher while she writes them for the child, verbalizing the words and explaining the mechanics of the writing. The use of spatial words such as "up," "down," "around," "in," "out," "straight," "curved," and numerous others should be used as frequently as possible by teachers when writing letters for these children. They not only give additional practice in hearing the words but give the child a spatial orientation as to what the body is doing in order to perform prescribed motoric responses. This will be discussed more in the chapter on writing and sensory motor development.

Since the story is written in the child's own words, he will be more inclined to remember it, and as the teacher prints the child's spoken words, the youngster becomes familiar with how the spoken word is represented in printed form. When he is able, the child in reading may wish to record, type, illustrate, write songs and poems about, or dramatize his stories. All these experiences give further practice in hearing, saying, and seeing his personal thoughts. Many times these children will enjoy using the same story and speculating on how it would have turned out different, if. . . . Suggestions may be made by the teacher, but the outcome should maintain the originality of the child. It is sometimes easiest to get children to think of the alternates by taking phrases of the story or pictures of the story and having the youngster sequence them. Through the use of the visual clues of the pictures they will often discover that if the pictures are arranged in another order the whole outcome might be different.

Weston Woods film strips supply what they call "tell back books" which are cartoonlike pictures which reproduce and tell a story about the film strips. Again, there are many possibilities in these filmstrips and the child should be involved in choosing those of interest to him. The process of reading is not all easy for him, and it may become impossible if he does not have the interest or the experiences to draw on.

Along with the development of stories, the children can create their own dictionaries from the words that are used in their stories. The child should type the word on one side of a card so that it appears as it most often would when he sees it in print and on the other side use a clue which he chooses to use.

The clue may be a picture, a configuration clue, or some irregular spelling of the word. What he chooses to use does not matter as long as it helps him to figure out the word without help when reviewing his words. Through the use of the cards the child can build sentences and poems that will vary the meaning from the original meaning in his stories. Keeping them in alphabetical order will give him practice in organizing and ordering his world.

All this can be developed from the child's own experiences. The task of the teacher is to provide the opportunity for the experiences and helpful ways for the child to remember those experiences. If they are really his own and original he will remember the words, be more anxious to share his stories with others, hear the stories of others, and most importantly, begin to build the all important sight vocabulary. Once the child has a substantial sight vocabulary and has had some success with reading, he is ready to approach the mechanics of reading. He might choose words that rhyme with his dictionary words. Categorizing words, choosing words that are all spatial, finding all the words that tell where, or when, or that name something are reading skills he will enjoy developing. Listing words that begin or end with a certain letter and then writing a story using them is another approach to mechanics of reading that might be used. Through all of this, the teacher is leading away from the original thoughts of the child to the meaning of whole words and to the placement of letters in those words. At the same time, she is illustrating the story as a series of thoughts expressed in units, the sentence as a series of word units, and the word as a series of letters.

REFERENCES

1. *Learning Methods Test*, Mills Center, Inc., 1512 E. Broward Blvd., Fort Lauderdale, FL, 33312.
2. *Sullivan Programmed Reading Series, 3rd Ed.* by M. W. Sullivan and C. D. Buchanan, McGraw Hill Publishing Co., 1244 Mark St., Bensenville, IL, 60106.

Chapter 8

THE SPATIAL WORLD OF
THE NATURAL CHILD

THE naturalistic mode of consciousness implies a highly developed awareness of sensory motor activity. The naturalistic child loves play, fantasy, and active experience. This mode of awareness sometimes precludes utilization of language constructs such as time, sequence, social responsibility, and general learning and behavioral organization. Children who experience this sort of neurological dominance find that thinking and focusing upon logical relationships and time-space organization is difficult and less than motivating because they must work so hard to concentrate on abstract operations. Further, as has been pointed out, these children often have some confusion in motoric organization and dominance in that they may tend to organize both left to right and right to left. Theirs is not a naturally organized world and if they are required to organize themselves in the conventional manner they may become confused. It is perfectly logical to them to work with their hands in whatever direction or manner that seems appropriate to them at the moment. Thus, writing and fine motor activities which involve sequential left to right organization are difficult and require special attention and practice if they are to learn the appropriate movements. In this chapter some of these difficulties will be explored and suggestions given for assisting such a child in learning basic movement patterns required in formal learning.

Language and Automation

Aside from the natural tendency to avoid formal motoric organization in a left to right fashion and the possibilities for crossed motoric and cerebral dominance patterns, the central issue in many of the children seen in the clinic is that of "automation." Automation, as described earlier, involves the buildup of specific motoric patterns through repetitious learning until they become "automatic." These patterns appear to be controlled by the sensory motor mechanism in the brain stem as described by Penfield. This concept was discussed in Chapter 2 and should be reviewed by the reader at this point. The central control mechanism in the sensory motor mechanism of the complex motoric patterns is activated through communication from conscious directions via the highest brain mechanism. Thus, when the child "consciously" initiates volitional behavior in motoric function, the sensory motor mechanism carries out the motoric function. This function may involve the simple act of writing a letter or a word or the complex act of moving through a series of motoric functions such as walking home from school. The ability of the sensory motor mechanism to initiate and carry through a complex act of motoric function cannot be underestimated.

The child, through early development and subsequent complex motoric learning, develops an extensive matrix of motoric behavior programs in the sensory motor mechanism which can be activated by the conscious stream of thought and carried out by the sensory motor mechanism. But the child must learn initial motoric movements and patterns prior to the eventual development of complex behavioral patterns. This facility is one of the most important motoric functions learned by the child.

As the child learns to walk, he must attend to his every movement, often failing in his judgements and falling to the floor. The same pattern of slow and careful direction of the motor movements can be observed from birth forward. In Ayres work it has been shown that the child not only must learn these motoric patterns carefully but basic postural reflex behaviors must be suppressed and overcome also before the child is able to master general balance and movements.[1] The child's attention to the motor patterns such as balance and walking involve "conscious" effort and practice in controlling the physiological system. In this case the child's conscious effort directly forwards information to the voluntary muscular system apparently training it as if it were some sort of "other" person. The child consciously trains and practices the motor system much as he learns to move toys and to play with "things." In a very real sense the child is internally visualizing and "thinking" his body through movement patterns he has seen others perform. It is much like the mental practice of the adult in learning skills of a sport. As the child practices these movements his conscious attention is directed toward the sensory motor mechanism. As the movements become more effective through trial and error, the child needs to direct less conscious attention to the movements. As the child learns balance and movement, he comes to consciously attend to the consequence of movements while sending messages to the sensory motor mechanism to carry out the movements. Initial sensory motor mechanism programs now come into use.

As the child develops during the first five years he creates an infinite number of motoric programs which he can use in a variety of situations. He no longer must attend to the actual direction of movements but, as was just stated, to the objectives of movements. Little difficulty may be noted until the Alpha child attempts to copy forms or specific symbols which require specific movement patterns in some directional orientation. When the natural child draws from his own orientation he may begin in any direction which pleases him. But copying a letter requires that he make that letter within specific directional orientation. The natural child may tend to work from right to left much like the left-handed child. Thus, when a "b" is presented to the child he will make a "d," and, for the first time, the natural child finds frustration in one of his most enjoyable functions, movement. He has never experienced any particular frustration in movement and suddenly he is faced with much confusion. He will now have to focus his conscious attention to the spatial nature of the form as well as to its directional and temporal characteristics. It must be made according to predetermined size, structure, direction, and sequence with other letters. The natural child is a free child and he expresses what pleases him. He cares little about convention, temporal orientation, size, or specific form. But now, with the introduction of formal instruction, he begins to struggle with the development of integrating language and space; it is not always a happy experience.

For the naturalistic child, then, initial formal educational experiences involve, for the first time, being confronted with definite directional and sequential ways of performing motorically. This left to right organization not only conflicts with the child's tendency to work from right to left motorically, but he may also organize his thoughts from right to left. For example, the child often believes that Tuesday comes "after" Wednesday. This tendency requires that the child consciously organize and "think" through such words and sequences which must proceed from left to right. This tendency to organize from right to left appears to be quite resistant to permanent change even though the child can eventually overcome it adequately in order to succeed in school. The child will have to have much practice in reading and writing in order to overcome his naturalistic tendency to organize from right to left. Further, the difficulty the child experiences will vary from child to child relative to the degree of right hemispheric tendencies existent in the system. The child with strong right hemispheric tendencies may functionally overcome this tendency but may revert when he is tired, under stress, or not attending well.

The teacher and the parent *must* grasp the issue involved in the natural child's difficulties in learning. We often have parents who come to us with children labeled as learning disabled, dyslexic, perceptually handicapped, or a host of others which they have difficulty understanding. Many of these parents state that their child has "always" been well coordinated and it is difficult for them to accept that their child can have a "perceptual-motor disability." In some cases, the parents do have a child who exhibits a syndrome of neurological dysfunction, but most often they have a child who has not "learned" specific directional or formalized fine motor movements while general coordination is quite good. There are a number of psychometrists and even psychologists working with schools who have been too conscientious and vigorous in their interest in adopting the whole learning disability phenomenon. Diagnosis of spatial disorders, perceptual handicaps, and specific learning disabilities have been given to children on the basis of the psychometrist's testing. However, the psychometrist or teacher who uses such a test and gives a diagnosis of a learning disability often has little or no idea of what it means or what to do about it. They too often have little knowledge of how children learn and particularly about the developmental range of behavioral possibilities which fall within the normal range. Subsequently, it is too much to hope that these individuals could possibly comprehend that a child is different developmentally but has no particular disorder or neurological dysfunction.

The natural child who is inclined toward motoric activity and who is generally well coordinated when he is initiating the movement will, if he has crossed motoric and cerebral dominance, have difficulty in learning to control his fine motor organization and spatial orientation within extremely defined limits of left to right organization. Thus, he has no difficulty in general coordination, and he does not actually have a perceptual problem or learning disability. These terms, in our work, are reserved for children who display actual neurological dysfunction. It is true that the natural child will reverse his letters, put "tails" on his diamond drawings, or attempt to read backward just as the child with an actual neurological dysfunction. But the natural child is having difficulty orienting in a world designed for a specifically structured individual, the right-handed person, while the neurologically damaged child performs in the same fashion because the central nervous system is incompetent and unable to process sensory information. While the resulting problems may appear similar, the two causal factors are significantly different and may require different approaches educationally. Our greatest concern is that the number of children brought to us who have some sort of actual neurological dysfunction, in comparison to those who are claimed to have such a problem, is so small as to render the notion of brain damage more a result of the examiner than of the child. Those children with actual brain dysfunction usually have many indicators of dysfunction, and most adults involved are aware of the disorder. In most cases, if the child is a natural child or simply a child with inadequate experience and development, we would not choose to call their "problem" a "disorder" at all.

In the following statements we want to outline some of the common problems faced by the naturalistic child and many other children in "normal" motoric and language development.

Poor Automation in Language-related Activities

While the natural child may be adequate in general coordination, establishing directional orientation for specific formal learning tasks will result in a variety of learning difficulties. Remember, the child can move and perform motoric activity adequately as long as he initiates the movement himself without external criteria for how that movement should be directed. In learning to make forms or letters, the Alpha child visually recognizes the structure of the form, but when he attempts to draw it according to specific directional orientation, he often finds that his hands appear to go "the wrong way." At a most basic level we can look at a cross and a square. The child may have some difficulty in making the forms with the proper or predetermined movements, such as left to right, but he is able to make these forms his own way, and the teacher may observe no difficulty unless she observes "how" he makes them. Further, these forms are usually mastered by the time the child is between the fifth and sixth year. There are several incorrect ways in which the immature or Alpha child may learn to make these drawings in his own way without undue concern by the teacher. He may draw two lines, one down and one from right to left, rather than left to right:
He may draw two lines vertically by turning the paper rather

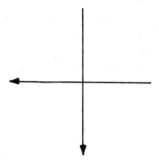

than one vertically and then one horizontally from left to right. (Rotate paper for line 2.)

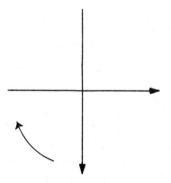

The Alpha Child may use the same methods for making the square; he does not draw a continuous line:

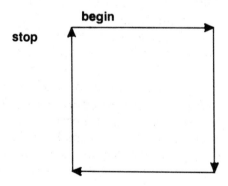

If the child does draw a square in a continuous line it will often go from right to left and top to bottom. But when he reaches the diamond he begins to have difficulty with direction and develops the classic soft neurological sign, "tails." Why does he do this? Because he is brain damaged? No. Because it is trial and error with a system that works backwards.

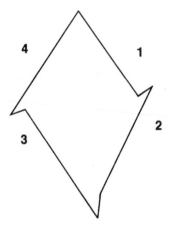

Here we have a diamond with tails. The brain damaged child will often repeat this form even with practice, and if he attains some degree of skill he will often lose it after some period of time. The Alpha child does it not because he has a defective visual and motoric function but because he is having difficulty coordinating his right to left orientation with the required left to right mode. The Alpha child begins line 1 and when reaching the first directional change he begins to draw the line when he realizes that he is going the wrong way. He simply reverses direction resulting in the first "tail" at the junction of lines 1 and 2. He repeats the same behavior at juncton 2 and 3. He is confused, for when he looks at the model of the diamond and tries to draw it he ends up going the wrong way. This is because he is operating on a right hemispheric right to left motoric function which is quite normal for him but is the opposite of the left hemisphere left to right neurological function. The Alpha child, with practice, eventually is able to master this problem by giving his sensory motor mechanism

specific training in performing the "opposite" motor movement for this particular sort of activity. He has to learn a reversal pattern in a system that is already programmed. While
the child can produce very elaborate drawings when he establishes his own direction, he now has to return to direct control
and monitoring the motor system. For a child who loved to
draw, making letters and forms is not much fun, but he is not
brain damaged; he is just different.

In summary, when the right hemisphere directs movements
or organizes sequential information, it naturally orients from
right to left just as the left hemisphere operates from left to
right. This phenomenon was discussed in Chapter 3. When an
individual, right- or left-handed, controls that hand by right
hemisphere orientation and direction, there will be a tendency
to orient right to left. As was mentioned earlier, it is possible
for the hand to be controlled by either hemisphere in either a
contralateral or ipsilateral fashion. The child with natural left-
handed control will tend to have the reversal tendency but so
will the right-handed child who controls the right hand with
the same side, or ipsilateral right hemisphere. Further, if the
right hemisphere is also the dominant mode of perceptual and
cognitive orientation, then the reversal tendency will be pro-
nounced. It is not enough to assume, then, that simply because
a child is or is not left-handed that the left hemisphere or right
is the major hemisphere. Hemispheric dominance must be established by a number of factors as pointed out in Chapter 4.

Cerebral Competition Can Retard Motoric Development

Following the verification of Geschwind and Levitsky[2] that
the left temporal plate is usually larger than the corresponding
area in the right temporal plate, it has been well established
that there is a genetic tendency toward language dominance in
the left hemisphere. Other researchers including Teszner[3] have
found that in fetal brains the left temporal plate was larger in
64 percent of the cases, in the right in 10 percent of the cases,
and equal in 26 percent of the cases. This research gives much
strength to the concept that the left hemisphere is genetically

the "major" hemisphere, since language plays such an important role in general behavioral competence. Since it is the temporal plate area in the left hemisphere which includes the speech, language organization, audition, and other important verbal functions, then an enlargement of this area in both fetal and adult brains suggests there is a natural tendency toward the left hemisphere assuming a major role in intelligent behavior. This also suggests that the left hemisphere is the "logical hemisphere to assume motoric control and general dominance in matters of cognitive and language organization or a sequential, left to right, perceptual, and cognitive organization.

If, as we have suggested here, there are individuals who tend to utilize a right hemispheric organization in motoric and cognitive function even though there is adequate language, then it is probable that an actual competitive force can exist between the right and the left hemisphere for control of the motoric and cognitive system. This can be resolved through developing different areas of dominance for each hemisphere. This, we suspect, is probable as case studies of children with right hemispheric behavioral tendencies are analyzed. For example, the child may develop adequate language ability in the natural left hemispheric structure but also develop general right hemispheric dominance in conscious functions. Such a child would be able to talk and express himself adequately, but he would avoid this behavior in favor of motoric and nonverbal behaviors such as building, active physical play, drawing, painting, engaging in much fantasy and day dreaming, music, sports, or simply watching television. The child often appears to be "in his own world" and to have difficulty with sequential tasks, attending to verbal presentations, organizing his work, and in certain math, spelling, reading, and writing activities. The formal learning environment for this child would present endless frustrations in that he would constantly be bombarded with requests to focus on language structure and organization. There would exist a competition between the socialized left hemisphere and social demands of the environment and his natural tendency to avoid language and engage in nonverbal activity.

This competition within the child is neurological (the natural tendency of the left hemisphere to control consciousness, along with the internal desire to engage in right hemispheric function) and social (as the demands of the teacher and parents for acceptable attention and effort in linguistic tasks). On one hand, the child may concentrate on left hemispheric function and be able, for a short period of time, to organize quite well. Eventually, the child may drift toward his naturalistic preference and end up making all sorts of directional and language mistakes in favor of the right to left organization of the naturalistic mode. It is of course, quite possible that the child is not trying and that he does have an emotional problem related to learning. But it is a situation in which the child could with proper assistance learn to organize his behavior if the teacher can assist him in modulating or resolving his motivation and emotional reasons for avoiding the task.

The following is a case study of a youngster seen in the clinic. James is not unlike many youngsters we have seen nor are the behaviors which brought about his referral.

> James was a happy child who often became discouraged by the unjust expectations he felt that teachers had for him. He was in the fourth grade in a private school when we saw him in the clinic. He had never been held back in school, and though it was only December his parents had already been informed that he should be held back next year because of his apparent immaturity. "Apparent immaturity" is a phrase we have come to expect in cases like James. The presenting problems to the school were as follows:
>
> *Reading:*
> Inability to complete assignments.
> Difficulty in reading comprehension.
> Reading level at early to middle third grade.
> Poor phonetic skills.
> *Spelling:*
> Inconsistant, with careless errors.
> *Writing:*
> Sloppy and obvious poor control and coordination.
> *Math:*

No great problem except getting assignments done.
Behavior:

Apparent lack of concern.

Inability to accept responsibility for work.

Liked by peers but tends to be easily led into pranks or
   unruly behavior, though he appears to be a "good" boy.

Not as well-developed physically as other boys his age.

James was nine years four months when he was seen in
February. He was somewhat young for his peer group since
he had started to school in the first grade at the age of five
and turned six in the middle of October. He had come to his
present school from another state, following completion of
the third grade. The parents reported that he had learned to
read many words by the time he was four. He enjoyed a
preschool in which he was enrolled between the ages of three
and five after which he entered a kindergarten in a private
school.

On the WISC-R Intelligence test, James scored the following levels of competence (scaled scores are used):

Information	11
Similarities	10
Arithmetic	12
Vocabulary	9
Comprehension	11
Verbal IQ	104
Picture Completion	9
Picture Arrangement	15
Block Design	16
Object Assembly	15
Coding	11
Performance IQ	122

Peabody Picture Vocabulary Test:

Verbal IQ	135

Wide Range Achievement Test:

Reading	5-1
Math	6-2
Spelling	3-2

Peabody Achievement Test:

Word recognition	6-1
Comprehension	5-8

Spache Diagnostic Scales:
 Word recognition   5-3
 Comprehension   5-0
Berry Developmental Test of Visual Motor Integration:
 Mental Age   10-8
Goodenough-Harris Drawing Test:
 Mental Age   11-0

James displayed poor organization on the Berry forms and required much time to complete them, making many erasures. His "draw a person" was quite elaborate and included much detail, action, and background. He enjoyed drawing and often did so in school.

When James was forced to perform through language functions in school he was operating in the average range of comprehension and skill. These language activities include attending to verbal information, organizing, reading assignments, answering questions, responding in written form, and completing assignments. Due to his tendency to want to daydream, to avoid organization, to draw, to watch other students, and to look at pictures in books, he had difficulty attending and following through on school tasks. Here is an example of how a competition exists between his own desire to succeed to school, his teachers' expectations, and his general tendency to drift into right hemispheric consciousness and activity. He could not, by his own effort, focus his attention or, at least, not in the manner which the teacher expected or for the required time. The results included all of the problems seen by the teachers. He did poorly in school and, to the teacher, would appear simply immature and not ready for learning which hopefully would be resolved by his having an extra year to mature. However, James was neither immature nor was he behind in learning skills. He was actually ahead in basic skill development but unable to use such skills in the manner expected by the school. What should be done with James? His was not a skill or maturation problem but one of attending and producing.

This was explained to the teachers. Their initial responses were complete agreement concerning the general notion that he was intelligent and complete disagreement that he was mature. Even though many suggestions were made for adapting James' curriculum, the school had decided that he should still be retained in the fourth grade. For this reason, the parents returned James to the public schools the following fall. Upon the principal's recommendation after reading the report and following an in-service school achievement evaluation, James entered the fifth grade. The school was an open school and utilized individually guided materials. James did well with support, structure, and contingency management. He did not repeat the fourth grade. He did become the star basketball player on the fifth grade team.

James' problems are not unusual in our case records, but the outcome is unusual in that most schools are able to assist the children once they understand how they function. In this case the private school was unable to adapt their program to fit the needs of the child. This is not the case in most private schools nor public schools, but when the teacher attempts to fit the child into arbitrary molds and when teacher expectations run counter to the developmental reality and needs of children, an inflexible situation is created. At the end of this chapter we will discuss the approaches used with James and other children like him which appear to display significant results. Our intent here was to illustrate how a child's own cerebral competition may create problems both for himself and the school.

We will, following the general tendency of neurological research, refer in our discussion to the major hemisphere as being the left hemisphere and the minor hemisphere as being the right hemisphere though it should be clear by now that this designation is more a genetic bias than it is a reality in general behavioral or learning style. In most individuals, the left hemisphere may be the major hemisphere relative to language function, but this need not imply that the child utilizes this hemisphere as the predominate mode of function.

Natural Children Often Exhibit Syndromes of Behavior Commonly Referred to as "Hyperactive"

Hyperactivity is a label which has come to be so popularized that few school personnel or parents have not heard it or read at least one article in a professional or popular publication concerning the syndrome. Hyperactivity within the clinical definition is a range of behaviors which includes short attention span, higher than average activity level, distractability, impulsiveness, and poor behavioral organization all of which are usually associated with some sort of neurological disorder. Such children are usually identified at a very young age by parents who are unable to deal with their incessant activity in the home. It is an obvious syndrome and one that usually requires little observation to recognize. There appears to be a difference between the "clinical" manifestations of hyperactivity and the use of the word to label overly active children in the public school. The present popular use of the term has reached levels where any child who does not attend well in school is labeled carelessly by teachers and parents as hyperactive. This often results in attempts to gain medication relief for the child and teacher for a disorder which may or may not involve actual neurological difficulties. This sort of practice can lead to a lack of understanding of the many other causes of distractability, which can include the teacher's own difficulties in instructional techniques or the parents' intolerance of particular child behaviors.

Hyperactivity, with the popularity of the term, has come to be utilized as part of "dyslexia" behavior characteristics, of characteristics included in many emotional-social difficulties, and even as the consequences of food coloring and additives in foods. All of these expanded popular definitions of hyperactivity have brought with them a great variety of medications, diets, special learning materials, and programs all proportedly effective in "treating" hyperactivity. The problem also has prompted some authors such as Bakwin and Bakwin[4] to distinguish between "clinical hyperactivity" and "developmental hyperactivity." Werry, following Bakwin and Bakwin's lead, elaborated characteristics of developmental hyperactivity to include overly active behavior in a school age child who exhibits no other evidence of neurological or mental disorders.[5] Thus, while there are children who appear to exhibit a variety of neurological causes for hyperactivity such as a means of reducing internal arousal,[6] seizure disorders stemming from temporal lobe lesions,[7] and disturbed diencephalic function,[8] most children referred do not exhibit such neurological manifestation. Developmental hyperactivity, then, provides a distinction between children with frank brain dysfunction and those who may be overly active and distractable due to a variety of nondysfunction disorders.

The indiscriminate use of various cerebral stimulants for children who do not exhibit actual neurological dysfunction may be quite questionable. Weiss et al. studied sixty-four hyperactive children in a five-year followup study.[9] In spite of substantial drug therapy, a significant proportion of these children manifested psychopathology five years later including antisocial behavior, emotional immaturity, and poor school achievement. Obviously, further studies of this sort are needed to truly assess the use of drugs with children who exhibit hyperactive syndromes and to achieve more accuracy in diagnosis of hyperactivity.

It is not our intent to propose a definition for hyperactivity or even engage in the extended arguments which surround the issue. We do propose that there is at least one fresh way of looking at the issue of distractability, impulsiveness, high activity level, and many of the other manifestations so commonly referred to as "hyperactive behavior." The natural child with his tendency to engage in nonverbal organization and his difficulty with language, time, and sequential organization often appears distractable, overly active, and impulsive. He tends to have difficulty with temporal organization due to his fixation on "now" oriented behaviors which often involve movement and activity. These behaviors, however, are as natural for him as the well-organized and sequential behaviors of the left minded or socialized child. What we have is a child who is unable, at worst, and unwilling, at best, to concentrate on organized language-based curricula imposed upon him in the public school classroom. His lack of organization is simply not consonant with the goals of the school, and he therefore appears hyperactive by the criteria of the school.

We must return to the probability that many of the natural children are quite at home with activity as long as they make the movement decisions. When these children must deal with temporal organization, left to right motoric organization, and sequential cause-related behavior, they become disoriented, disorganized, and confused giving the impression of perceptual or neurological difficulties. Further, their lack of adequate, organized motoric programming and automation make it difficult for them to operate under environmentally predetermined structures. It is interesting that many of these children, if placed in an individually guided program or in an open school program, are less likely to be perceived by the teacher as hyperactive. The freedom of movement and the significant level of personal directedness allow the children to deal with the school environment.

In the latter section of this chapter we will present some contingency approaches for assisting these children in the school environment. Even though they have difficulty with organization, this does not imply that they should not learn, within their individual capacity, to conform and to deal with the structure of school-related learning. We need to organize their world with understanding and tolerance for their natural perceptual world, gently moving them toward effective learning behaviors while not destroying their curiosity and creativity.

The Natural Child Often Displays Temporal-Spatial Integration Difficulties

The relationship between spatial organization and time concepts has already been discussed in earlier chapters. Temporal and spatial integration are required for the child to organize his world and his behavior. The natural child, with his tendency to spatialize his world without regard for time concepts can and often does suffer devastating consequences to his learning capacities. It is important though to make a distinction between the child who has neurological dysfunction, i.e. significant brain damage which prevents learning either spatial or language functions, and the natural child who, though he has no significant damage, prefers to orient primarily on a spatial bias while disregarding temporal aspects of his environment. The natural child, in this case, is assumed to have at least average or higher language capacity but, because of significantly higher spatial capacity, prefers spatial organization to temporal function. This preference may be due to higher capacities, but it may also be a consequence of a lack of language training or opportunity, emotional components which press the child to avoid temporal behavior, or other environmental conditions which inhibit language function. The natural child requires constant support and encouragement in language-temporal function to avoid the over spatialization orientation and to develop adequate language development and temporal-spatial integration. The following behaviors are typical of the child who avoids temporal activity:

a. Poor sequential organization; difficulties in remembering sequence of days of the week, months of the year, or the alphabet and numbers.
b. Difficulty in seeing behavioral consequences of personal behavior, resulting in poor responsibilty and recognition of the needs of others.
c. Difficulty in organizing and following through on educational tasks, being easily distracted.
d. Inability to recall a sequence of directions or to follow them in the proper order.
e. Tendency to reverse order of letters in spelling.
f. Impulsive behavior; need for immediate gratification.
g. Difficulty in understanding social rules.
h. Tendency to daydream.
i. Difficulty in learning to tell time.
j. Continued tendency to word call in reading without comprehension and difficulty in maintaining adequate scanning and tracking skills in reading.
k. Difficulty in learning complex motoric movements through modeling.
l. Difficulty in rhythmatic activities.

These difficulties, as may be recognized, are often also characteristics of the child with some sort of learning disability or frank brain damage. But the natural child can learn these functions through structured direction, while for the brain damaged child such learning continues to be difficult.

In our work with children it seems appropriate to assume that spatial development precedes temporal development. This is somewhat evident in that temporal function involves recognition and awareness of the passing of time, awareness of past, present, and future, and the ability to predict or expect certain outcomes or events on the basis of past or present behavior. These abilities depend upon maturation and appear in the form of conservation, pointed out by Piaget, when the child is able to understand that objects hidden from view or which have passed from view still exist. The child's ability to understand the existence of objects and events outside of his spatial-sensory awareness involves temporal organization. The child is able to understand that matter remains the same even though they change shape. When the child views a number of objects he is able to conserve the concept of their quantity even though they assume different spatial orders. Such behavior gives rise to deductive and inductive behavior based on memory of past events and the nature of things. These skills involve an integration of spatial sensory information and temporal information. Spatial memory alone would not serve to organize and serialize information since it is within left hemispheric function that sequential memory is developed. These abilities are dependent upon sophisticated temporal-spatial integration. At a more elementary and practical level, the integration of space and time have important implication for the child's behavior.[10]

Gravity provides for the child a continuous and stable reference point in space. During the first few months of motor spatial learning, the child struggles with control of his body and with movement in relation to the stress of gravity. As he learns movement patterns which enable him to propel his body he also learns to move parts of his body in directions to the left and right, fore and aft. These movements provide an additional awareness of space beyond that provided by gravity. Basic movement patterns of the child are eventuated into conscious awareness of directions. In much of the literature (Kephart)[11] concerning motor-spatial development the internal consciousness of left and right, fore and aft, and up and down are described as "laterality." This internal awareness is externalized to the environment so that the child recognizes directions around him in relation to his internal reference, an ability called "directionality." As objects move across the child's visual field he turns his head and follows them. In infancy the most natural movement appears to be up and down, and it is this movement which is first placed into the internal reference of laterality and directionality.

As the infant struggles to lift his head and then his upper torso, he learns to work against gravity and he also exercises a basic movement pattern related to the up and down movement. He eventually overcomes basic postural reflexes and is able to move himself in this up and down fashion along with turning his head and finally moving each arm or leg separately. As he begins to move different parts of his body, he also begins to learn left, right, forward, and backward movements. He listens to sounds in his environment and watches objects move about him, learning more and more intricate visual and motor movements in the three major planes of spatial orientation. It is this early spatial-motor and sensory-motor behavior which lays the basis for the infant's recognition of various points in space.

As the child matures through the first three years of life, he learns words to associate with various movements and points in space which he has already come to know as a natural spatial world. Verbal instructions such as "Come here," "Go into the house," "Go up to bed," and "Open the door," all are examples of "naming" spatial-motor acts and creating an abstraction of the spatial-motor world. With recognition of day and night comes temporal passing of time which is replaced with today, tomorrow, and yesterday. This morning and this afternoon become more sophisticated concepts of language-spatial reality for the child just as "in a few minutes," "a little while," "very soon," "not for a long time," and "not until tomorrow." As the child learns more and more about the passing of time through relating it with concrete experiences of day, night, afternoon, evening, morning, he is able to understand more subtle meanings such as Monday, Saturday, spring, winter, and eventually, minutes and hours which come to be represented by the abstract symbols (numbers) appearing on a clock. As the child matures and substitutes abstract language and language concepts for concrete sensory-motor experiences, he begins to integrate temporal and spatial learning. It is essential to understand that temporalizing sensory-motor experiences requires that the child learn the abstractions of language so that he can have some finite filing system for reference. Words come to represent in the abstract those concrete experiences which he accumulated during early sensory motor and spatial experience. It is this maturation and learning from concrete to abstraction which will allow the child to organize his behavior, to predict events that are not now occurring, and to reflect on past experiences. It is essential that the child eventually learn language and all of its designating and defining indicators in order to formalize his thought. The spatial world provides the initial concrete experience upon which memory and abstract thinking can be built.

While it is not always the case, most of us tend to identify time as passing "before us" from left to right. We have found some individuals who use a variation of this theme but in most cases the passing of time is "visualized" as moving in some direction in relation to our spatial orientation. In an earlier discussion we suggested that most individuals appear to think of the past as existing in some area to the left and the future as existing somewhere to the right. Thus, time is usually understood as moving left to right. This is consistent with the left hemispheric tendency to organize from left to right. However, the natural child may not experience or learn time in this fashion.

The natural child often exhibits difficulty with them in that he tends to fixate in his perceptual processes much more on the moment or, in difficult cases, he may organize time in a right to left fashion. He is able to learn left to right conceptualization, but he often has the tendency to organize from right to left. This tendency, either to organize only on the present or from right to left can cause significant difficulties in his general learning behavior. Words are written from left to right in a sequence of some definite form. This may appear backward to the natural child, and he may display many difficulties in learning to write or read, such as reversing letters, reversing the order of letters in a word, or tending to look for words on a page in a disorganized fashion, often losing his place. Even when he does think in an appropriate left to right manner he may end up writing in the reverse order. This tendency is caused by the overriding dominance of right hemispheric direction even though the child may be concentrating on left hemispheric organization.

The natural child, due to his difficulty in organizing time and temporal concepts in the appropriate sequence or structure, may also find it too difficult to attempt to understand how to tell time. It is so difficult for him to conceptualize time or temporal left to right patterns that he simply avoids them, with the result that he is much later than other children in learning to tell time. Along with this difficulty he also appears to forget or to avoid using time concepts in his behavior. He does not think of consequences and, therefore, is often unable to avoid difficulties with rules. The natural child often has difficulties in specific recall of names, dates, and other information of a specific nature. In that he is not using language well as a temporal filing system, he has difficulty using words to recall specific data. It is not that he does not know the information but simply that he has not developed and organized a method of recalling it.

Special attention has to be given to the natural child in learning to tell time, in grasping specific abstractions concerning temporal events, and in acquiring the ability to see past-present-future relationships.

If we think of rhythmatic behavior as a combination of temporal and spatial-motor behavior, it is possible that the natural child will have trouble learning complex motoric patterns if they must follow predetermined patterns of movement. He may be able to run, jump, and perform many excellent and well-coordinated movements as long as he is initiating them. As in modeling the behavior of others or learning an externally imposed pattern of movement, he has to organize himself internally to match an external pattern. When the child is forced to learn movements from external cues, all of the problems in directionality and spatial organization become apparent. This is why so many of these children appear generally well coordinated but often have coordination problems in a structured learning environment. Many children brought to the clinic are described by the parents as very well coordinated, and they are surprised when we tell them that they have difficulty in fine motor and externally directed movement patterns.

Natural Children Often Enjoy and Display High Skill in Areas Such as Drawing or Painting, Athletics, Construction, Play and Fantasy, Animals, and Music

Many natural children display an interest in drawing and painting very early. They love to make pictures, though at early stages of development the adult may have difficulty in understanding what the pictures are. The same child may have difficulty learning his letters or drawing a specific form designated by the adult. Their fascination with spatial elements and movement, a right hemispheric function, is given expression in their own egocentric manner without regard to convention or learning expectations. At other times, a child may enjoy block play, building things with father's tools, or simply piling everything in the room into one big and glorious heap which he labels his house. Again, because these children pay little attention to convention and organized learning, they often appear totally disorganized. Yet, in the context of their own immediate and rich fantasy world, all of their behavior seems perfectly logical to them. This spatial orientation often gives rise to unique patterns of behavior which may be described as creative when these children are small and disorganized when they enter school. The natural child is one who finds his own spatial world more interesting than the logical world demanded by the adults about him. He may enjoy physical activities and learning to play physical games. Many of these children become advocates of sports and games early, spending hours practicing movements and plays in which they can express their natural tendency to move and to involve themselves in concrete activity.

Natural children often are great pet enthusiasts, for animals fit well into their nonverbal communication of emotion and behavior. They form relationships easily with animals and enjoy their pets but, as many parents learn, they forget to feed them and to care properly for their needs. The routine and organized care required of animals is often beyond their ability, though they love and enjoy their pets nearly as much as their friends. Some of these children even prefer their pets to friends or other members of the family, for animals make few demands on a child's logic or order. In many ways, though it sounds cruel, animals think more like the natural child than do most playmates or adults. Animals will love you even if you ignore them for brief periods, and they do not demand that you account for your behavior. A good dog will tolerate much rough play from an overactive boy one moment and be ready to forgive in a moment when he wants to curl up on the floor for a short nap.

Natural children often fall easily into disorganized expression in response to music. They may love music and become quite attached to their favorite song even though they rebel at attempts to encourage them to learn to play an instrument or a specific song. They may pound on the piano for hours for their own enjoyment but formal lessons are met with resistance, if not outright hostility. All of these patterns of behavior are quite confusing to adults for they seem contradictory. A child may love music but refuse to learn a song. He may draw for an hour but refuse to draw as the adult wants him to. He may make a terrible fuss about getting a pet and then appear to care little for him. He may want to throw the ball endlessly with Dad and become angry when Dad tries to get him to throw it "correctly." The parents may buy an expensive set of blocks and toys because the child loves to build things, while he may prefer old boxes and "junk." The energies and temperament of the right hemispheric child are difficult for socialized and organized parents and teachers until the adults learn that the natural child must be gently encouraged into organized patterns of behavior and, at the same time, accept his continued resistance to such organization. The natural child is the dreamer and the unchained mind of creative youth. Natural adults grow up slowly and many never do, according to friends and family.

Management Principles

In the following pages the reader will be given some general teaching and behavioral management principles to be used with the natural child. Excellent books on perceptual motor development, creativity, and formal learning materials are listed in the references at the end of the chapter. The authors felt no need to duplicate such materials here. However, there are many basic principles which appear important in guiding the teacher and parent in working with these children which are not included in most books on development and learning. However, most authors do not know the Alpha child.

The teacher needs guidelines for working with the Alpha child, recognizing at the same time that such direction is never conclusive for it is from the everyday interaction with the natural child that the teacher must take cues as to how and when to meet specific needs of the child. The following general principles and activities should guide the teacher's interaction with the natural child, but by and large, the teacher will need to develop and alter such activities to fit the learning situation and the student's needs. What will work with one child will not be successful for another, and often, the same child will respond inconsistently to the same stimuli.

The Natural Child Requires Much Repetition and Practice in Basic Motoric Skills to Assure, as Much as Possible, Automation

In kindergarten and first grade the teacher must assure that the natural child learns to produce basic forms and then letters or numbers without hesitation or confusion. For these young children, who have difficulty with automation, repetition is the key to development of a nonconscious and automatic fine motor productive ability in relation to letters and words. Many professionals who work with children having perceptual handicaps have traditionally attempted to break down the skill tasks into their component parts and practiced the specific parts of the skill. For example, a child who reverses letters will often be diagnosed as having a "directional" or "spatial" disorder and specific balance and directional activities will be introduced in order to develop "directionality" after which the letters and various activities requiring this function will be learned. While this may be an accurate assessment of the problem and solution for the child with neurological dysfunction, it is not particularly appropriate for the natural child. The natural child, while he may have difficulties such as reversing letters, is not usually doing so because of poor directionality. The teacher should remember that the natural child has difficulties with direction due to a competing dominance between hemispheres and not particularly because there is a dysfunction. Further, the natural child tends to learn, like athletes, through comprehension and practice of an integrated movement pattern. Because of these factors the natural child should be taught fine motor and specific letter/number patterns through a holistic approach. This approach combines both language and spatial comprehension by verbally assisting the child in understanding the completed task. The task may be learning a forward roll, writing a series of letters, or spelling a word. The integrated and whole movement pattern should be demonstrated several times for the child as the teacher points out major characteristics of the movements or the completed product. Many specialists in the field of developmental disorders (such as learning disabilities) often advocate that children learn very specific aspects of a movement pattern prior to utilizing that pattern in some meaningful whole. The authors suggest that the child, particularly the natural child, will attempt to learn salient characteristics of a task rather than focusing upon a sequential and part-to-part structure as is often the case. Perhaps one of the most effective guides for this sort of specific instruction is given by Annabelle Markoff in her book *Teaching Low Achieving Children.*[12]

One of the major difficulties the natural child faces is concentrating on specific aspects of learning tasks. In teaching the natural child, tasks should be presented first in their entirety and then broken into parts for reinforcement. Again, as in the case of reading, the child is taken through the process of introduction of the total task and then to the individual parts.

Another aspect of recent teaching methodology in education which has provided some difficulty for the natural child is the philosophy and method of teaching part to whole without teaching such skills within meaningful units. For example, in learning to write a particular letter the natural child should learn the whole movement first and then practice specific aspects of the movement. More importantly though, the child should be given words and even sentences which utilize the skill within a meaningful whole. One of the most flagrant examples of "perceptual training" without meaning is that of teaching eye tracking through mechanical devices or some of the series in which the child counts letters across a line of print. These activities often improve visual tracking temporarily but, due to the fact that the skill is learned without any meaningful context, the skill often is lost rapidly. If the child is given a task in which the tracking involves some more general and meaningful function, then the skill appears to be retained longer. For example, reading itself is often an excellent eye movement training program. The child is asked to read a story which is within or even below his level of instruction. If he does not know a word he is given the word so that he can continue to read without hesitation. This causes the child to continue reading aloud across the page and, in the process, to practice eye movements, fixations, and efficiency. The task involves something for which the movements have meaning, reading.

Many motoric exercises are taught in very fragmented activities in order to teach the child each part, with the hope that he will combine them. Worse, some of these exercises, such as walking across the walking board, involve no meaningful goal except to very young children or to children with physical handicaps. For the natural child, the problem is integration

and efficiency of movement and therefore integrated and meaningful activities which include specific goals in motoric development are desired. This is why learning stunts on the
trampoline are so much more efficient than the more fragmented exercises. Gymnastics is by far a better perceptual and
motoric training program than the more clinical perceptual
motor training exercises. For the natural child, then, fine motor
and gross motor activities should be offered repeatedly and
within generalized and meaningful exercises that result in functional skills rather than meaningless and purposeless exercises.

Attention and Concentration Should Be Taught Through and Reinforced by Language

One of our earlier discussions pointed out that an individual
may be conscious within right or left hemisphere function.
When the young child daydreams and lets his mind wander, he
is usually conscious in creative and diverse awareness of his
own fantasies. While this is a very worthwhile and enjoyable
activity, it does not contain the sort of conscious activity which
is associated with attention in school. When the child is aware
of his responsibility to complete an educational task and when
he sequences his behavior in the proper direction and rate so
that the assignment is carried through, then he is functioning
within left hemispheric consciousness. Most natural children
can be forced into social consciousness simply through demanding that they attend to language. As we have mentioned
before, the natural children, the "dreamers," do not avoid logical and organized thinking on purpose, it is simply a matter of
what is the most enjoyable to the child. Language and logic are
not avoided, they simply are not "thought" of because they are
less enjoyable. Thus, with the natural child during a specific
learning task, the teacher or tutor must constantly call the
child's attention to the task through verbal directions and reinforcement. For the natural child reading aloud, verbally describing what he is doing, and even subvocalization during
silent reading all provide left hemispheric stimulation with
resultant concentration on the task. When the natural child

ceases to monitor his behavior verbally, he begins to drift into "alpha behavior" which is nondirectional, disorganized, impulsive, and fantasy oriented. Because of the natural child's strong right hemispheric tendency, he is very vulnerable to external nonverbal stimuli. Music, animal sounds or unusual nonverbal sounds, tactile sensations, color, and other environmental sensory information are examples of nonverbal stimuli he processes so easily. Such information can be stimulus for fantasy which commences nearly without the child's "conscious" effort.

The natural child can learn organization and he is able to sequence information, but constant language stimulation and learning is a must if he is not to drift away into his own world where all things can *be* simply because they *are* or because they delight. It is the natural child who so desperately needs the teacher in his world. In today's technological, individualized, teaching kit classroom, the child often loses the personalized and language interactive approach of yesterday's teacher. This may be a significant contributing factor to the number of distractable and even hyperactive children. Many children do not socialize easily, including the natural child who already has a neurological prerogative opposed to organization. For all of those young children who need the constant stimulation and organizing function of an adult during their younger years, today's schools and preschools may pose an impossible dilemma. The external control of an adult interacting with the child during the first seven or eight years, as in yesterday's family and early school experience, most likely provided the ingredient missing in much of today's society. Many children now enter preschools and day care centers where they do not receive adequate adult attention or direction, and they are unable to develop internally. During early school years, these children develop neurologically, academically, and socially as confused, undirected, and often fearful youngsters. By the time these children are in the second or third grade they are hopelessly lost and unable to direct themselves. They simply have not had enough adult supervision and direction to internalize the language and social structure required for effective attention and concentration. The natural child may be totally lost by this grade level unless we can intervene once more and recognize that teachers are more significant than books or kits.

The natural child must be given excessive amounts of teacher direction and interaction to stimulate and even force him into language-based organization and awareness. Learning to direct attention, like learning to walk, is not something that just happens; the child has to practice.

Relaxation exercises have been very successful with many distractable children in assisting them to learn to concentrate. These activities should occur at specific periods each day when every child is given, usually in a group, practice in how to make their bodies totally relaxed. The children are asked to lie on the floor and the teacher slowly takes the group through a series of activities which teaches them to first relax their heads, necks, and shoulders, their arms and legs, their feet and hands, and so on until they become completely limp and relaxed. There have been some articles concerning the relaxation approach in professional journals. Oddly enough, this practice of relaxing the body has the effect of improving concentration. In some countries in Europe, researchers have found that adults can learn more easily and efficiently if they assume relaxed postures and even appear not to attend to the verbal presentations.

The dynamics of psychoneurological function which causes this increase in attention and concentration while seemingly doing just the opposite is not so difficult to understand when one considers hemisphericity. The relaxation activity involves language concentration and control of the muscular system along with increasingly left hemispheric stimulation of the right hemisphere. The right hemisphere, as has been pointed out, appears to be closely aligned to nonverbal and motoric movements. If, through left hemispheric stimulation (concentration on the body), the individual can stimulate the right hemisphere to develop more control of the body system, an interhemispheric cooperation is developed whereby the right hemisphere develops and learns how to "control" the body system while the left engages in language learning without the distracting movement and activity of the opposing hemisphere. The competition theory concerning hemispheric function is somewhat controversial, but the discussion here recognizes the theory that when both hemispheres are busy processing the same information in different ways, or when each hemisphere is separately engaging in some sort of activity, these activities may cause interference in one or both of the hemispheres. This confusion usually results in a lack of direction by the child and random or impulsive behavior since his consciousness is drifting from one mode to the other without any strong preference or reason to concentrate on one or the other. It is as if the two computers are continuing to process information separately and causing each other interference while the child's consciousness is "out to lunch," so to speak. Relaxation teaches the child to focus his attention and to control the nature of hemispheric activity. This is not an easy task, for many adults find it hard to relax or to maintain their attention.

Attention must be developed then through training and constant direction until such time as he is able to modulate his own behavior and accept responsiblity for his own organization. Simply demanding that he do so, without the appropriate teacher direction and child learning, is like asking a physically handicapped child to suddenly get up and walk.

The Natural Child Needs Effective Behavioral Limits Within Structured Learning Environments and Supportive, Constant, and Definitive Limits at Home

How does the child learn responsibility? When does it begin, this development of responsibility, and by what mysterious process does one child develop responsibility and another not do so? There are many answers to these questions, each slightly different depending upon the child and the circumstances, but there are at least some general principles involved in learning personal control and responsibility. The following list is suggestive of many of the reasons children develop responsible behavior and the basis upon which such behavior is achieved.

a. Children model the adults and peers about them to learn early social behaviors.
b. Children learn personal responsibility through response to rewards and punishment given for acceptable and unacceptable behavior.
c. Children develop self-concept and social consciousness through the verbal values they are taught and which they apply to themselves as a means of measuring self-worth.
d. Children imitate appropriate social behaviors in order to gain love and acceptance from adults and peers.
e. Children behave in socially responsible ways based on the development of trust in others and the willingness to accept direction and limitations from those they trust and love.
f. Children develop responsible behaviors for reasons of security and safety; appropriate behaviors assure the protection of adults.
g. Children eventually internalize the values and behaviors of peer and adult models as their own values and, thereby, accept such values as their own.

Why are responsible behaviors so important to the child? Aside from the rewards and increased self-esteem which comes to well-behaved and directed children, the child learns to organize himself in appropriate ways to learn and to interact with others socially.

The relationship of socialization and values to the behavioral organization of the child is not clearly seen by many adults. It is often the child who is seen as "hyperactive" or "hyperkinetic" who is not internalizing or learning social behaviors. The contemporary society is experiencing what appears to be an increase in the number of children who appear overly active and unable to control their behavior. These children, aside from being extremely active, are often unable to relate to other children easily, are impulsive, disorganized, unmethodical, and difficult to manage both at home and school. Many reasons have been given for this behavior including neurological dysfunction, diet, artificial food colorings and additives, and emotional disorders. The authors agree that many children exhibit allergic reactions to foods, do exhibit special neurological problems, and often in some way are the victims of environmental insult which produces an inability to concentrate and control behavior. Unfortunately, in reality hyperactive behavior is most likely a cumulative effect of several problems and most often not the result of any one difficulty. Further, many children, perhaps most children, appear to exhibit the hyperactive syndrome, not so much due to any of these causes as to poor parental management of the child during the first five years.

In a review of many children referred to the authors' clinic, some interesting characteristics were seen as somewhat common among children who were referred for hyperactivity. The following characteristics were often seen.

a. The children were almost always boys who were displaying not only very active behavior but a high degree of ego centered and deterministic behavior.
b. In most cases there was evidence of poor parental limit-setting on the behavior of the child and the parents felt uncertain as to how the best approach to the child might be developed. There was evidence of inconsistency between parents in their discipline and limit-setting approaches.
c. In most cases there was encouragement of the typical boy aggressiveness on one hand and a subsequent rejection of the child for displaying such behavior, suggesting that the child received very inconsistent messages concerning how he should behave.
d. There was a high degree of verbal interaction between child and parents. This interaction tended to be both of a stimulating and challenging nature and one that encouraged the child to engage in some negativistic verbal patterns with adults without disciplinary action.
e. Most often the parents felt strongly about being open and democratic with their child in matters of conflict and attempted to take a reasoning approach as opposed to a more authoritarian or punitive approach in management.
f. In many of the cases there was evidence of high levels of stimulation; sports, television, community activities, play-

mates, toys, and special program participation by the children.

These characteristics are not presented to suggest that parental management techniques are the basic cause of all hyperactivity but rather to point out that in a majority of cases referred by parents, school, and physicians the number of children with neurological or physiological syndromes was far less than those who appeared capable of personal control but for a number of reasons did not seem to be willing to limit their own behavior. For this larger number of children, the basic cause of the hyperactive behavior was seen as parental and developmental difficulties in learning. It is suggested then that many children do not learn the behaviors associated with developing directed and responsible behavior. In the foregoing examples it would appear that the child did not or was unable to, due to maturation, learn through the parenting style presented by the parents. While the parents were generally well-meaning and concerned parents, their overstimulation and liberalization of the home environment tended to produce a crisis for the child who needed consistent and external controls. In the normal process of socialization, the child models his parents and responds to their direction. When parents attempt to force too much responsibility on the child too early, he may tend to develop some degree of panic and even anger resulting in a lack of responsible behaviors. This effect appears to be the opposite of that intended by the well-meaning parents.

In this sort of parent environment the natural child may experience even more difficulties. The natural child tends to disregard others, pay too little attention to verbal suggestions and interaction, does not consciously attend to the values of his peers, and may often become somewhat oblivious to the social world about him.

Just as the typical child may have difficulty in the overly permissive environment, the natural child may develop similar behaviors as a consequence of poor verbal attention. Thus, natural children often exhibit many of the same behaviors as the hyperactive child not so much due to parenting style as to his own tendency to avoid and disregard verbal instructions.

The natural child may exhibit these characteristics in both an authoritarian and a permissive environment but certainly the permissive environment stimulates the very difficulties the natural child tends to exhibit in any case.

Because the natural child is so preoccupied with things, with doing what pleases him and avoiding responsibility, and often separating himself from peer social environments, the early childhood environment and the eventual school environment must provide good limits and definite followup by adults to assure completion of assignments or tasks. Yet, this structure must be applied with sympathetic understanding that the child is not intentionally avoiding his responsibility. He simply does not think about it. It is true that the natural child may be very deterministic, but his behavior must be met with firm and sympathetic limits by the adult. There has to be give and take and at times it may be more important for the child's general welfare to give in and let him take his own direction. But he should always be brought back to task both at home and in school. Remember the natural child is listening to a different drummer and while we are attempting to direct him toward social responsibility we do not want to crush his potentially creative and individualistic personality. It is a difficult task for both parents and teachers and tests to the limit our real capacity to be teachers and parents.

Understanding of Time and Sequence Will Be a Continual Problem for the Natural Child and Extra Attention Must Be Given to This Special Need

During early learning tasks, as has been discussed, there is a general tendency to reverse letters and numbers in motoric confusion. This directional problem also affects the child's ability to understand time and temporal sequences. We have discussed the tendency of natural children to expect Tuesday to come after Wednesday, March to come before February, or nine to come after ten. These are all examples of a "conceptual directional" problem in which the child organizes time and sequence with the same difficulty that he finds in writing letters in the correct direction. Because of the competition between the hemispheres or due to dissonance within hemispheric function, the child has difficulty maintaining a stable directional reference point both for motoric and conceptual functions. To avoid the entire issue of time and sequence the child simply avoids learning or thinking in directional terms, he avoids thinking of time.

The natural child, in his quest to avoid the bothersome nature of time, often pays little attention to what time is, how long he may stay at a friend's house, or comprehending exactly what his mother's demand to clean up his room "later" means. "Later" is, in fact, the same as "never" since there is no means for the timeless, natural child to predict later. Not only do these children often learn to tell time on the clock late in their development, they often use gross characteristics to tell time. It is twelve o'clock when the little hand points to the twelve. Of course, not paying attention to the minute hand can cause some problems in that the child is usually from five minutes to twenty-five minutes off either way since he ignores the minute hand. When he finally learns to use the minute hand he still appears to pay little attention to the clock, and one does not do so well in telling time if one avoids looking at the clock. Digital watches, needless to say, have, along with the calculator, freed many natural children from the problem altogether.

The parent and teacher must understand that the natural child requires very specific directions and each direction should be given for immediate execution. He should be told to "clean up your room now" rather than "later." The child cannot work on his homework or seat work for twenty minutes, he has to work on it until he is done, and his progress should be checked every five minutes to make sure he is continuing to work and has not drifted off to some castle in his fantasy sky. It is tiresome for the adult, and the teacher should continue her efforts to teach time and organization. It should be remembered that the natural child, throughout his life, will have a tendency to avoid time and, if he or she is lucky, he will always have a partner or a spouse who will somehow continue, like the teacher and parent, to program his or her life according to standard central time. If we accept this difference in the natural child, it becomes no less difficult but at least maybe a little less tiring.

Doctor Oppenhiemer, driving to his office one day, found that he had absent-mindedly driven his car up the steps of the local library. Fortunately, the jolting of the car shook him back into time and space before he went through the front door. This is a constant difficulty for the natural Alpha child. His mind wanders while his world attempts to keep his attention firmly and responsibly on the present. The natural children should take heart in Thomas Edison who, caught in the creative and timeless world of inventiveness, finally was excluded from school because of his inability to follow directions, to complete his assignments, or attend to the present time. His mind was always off somewhere thinking and planning. Only when he needed information did he turn his attention to books. Once, when he needed some specific information from the library, he not only read the books he needed, but read all of them in the library. Small wonder, driven by a need to know information that fed his creative mind, that he found the nouns and adjectives of the fourth grade reader somewhat unstimulating.

For the parent or teacher of the natural child it is a life-long task to try to give the child as much structure as he can tolerate. Yet, if the child is learning, if he truly loves to create, to build, and to understand, then we must also compromise and attempt to give his curious mind room to grow so that someday we might benefit from something that comes from that wandering and creative mind.

Peer Group Associations Should Be Encouraged Along with Verbal Reinforcement of Peer Relationship Concepts

Peer relationships can be difficult for the natural child. The creative and nonverbal child often has a high need to express himself, to share his feelings, thoughts, and needs. But, due to the difficulty which words present to the creative, nonverbal individual, it is always difficult to share feelings verbally. Thus, the nonverbal child often turns to his creative abilities to express himself indirectly to others. This expression can take the form of physical activities such as sports, dance, art, or some other creative art form and are extremely important to the natural child, for the products of his effort, whether excellence in a sports activity, a painting or sculpture, or playing a musical instrument, are expressions of himself. These expressions are intensely personal and a way of sharing with others some of what he feels and experiences in his world. Unfortunately, these expressions too often are not understood nor appreciated by the highly verbal society, and the needed reinforcement does not materialize, leaving the natural child feeling rejected and lonely. We should not expect that highly verbal people who must evaluate everything for its practical value rather than its aesthetic value will be able to appreciate an abstract art form. Verbal individuals simply are not always able to "tune in" to the inner expressions of emotion and feeling that are so much a part of the natural child's life. This communication difficulty often leaves the natural child frustrated and even angry with others. Sometimes, natural children will be quick to become angry and respond to their world with overt aggression or withdrawal which puzzles the verbal individual. This is why teachers and parents should take nonverbal activity of the natural child very seriously and encourage the child to attempt to verbalize what their work means, what they feel about what they have created, and encourage them to explore words as a means of expressing themselves. A high degree of verbal practice is required for the natural child if he is to learn how to use the conventional mode of communication along with his naturalistic communication patterns.

Young naturalistic children should be encouraged to listen, to tell stories, to explain things they have heard, and to reexpress in their own words things they have learned. In elementary school, creative writing is very important not only as a means of reinforcing poor writing skill but also in developing the written form of expression.

The difficulties which natural children display in communication bring about one of their most frustrating experiences, difficulties in getting along with groups of peers. The natural child often finds it difficult to interact with other children successfully due to their inability to objectify their own and others' behavior. Too often the natural child with his tendency to view his world from an egocentric stance is unable to see how others feel, to share and cooperate, to give up his own goals in favor of group determined goals. Teachers and parents alike have to continuously point out to the natural child his role in relationships and help him think through and verbalize alternate strategies in getting along with others. Reality therapy, transactional analysis, and other contemporary processes of assisting individuals in understanding interpersonal relationships and communication are excellent approaches with the natural child and can be used by both parents and teachers.

Conversely, the natural child, while inhibited in verbal communication, may also find that the typical verbal child is inhibited in creative expressive abilities. Movement activities such as physical games and dances, art and music activities, creative story telling or writing, games that teach creative problem solving, and openness in emotional or affective expression are all activities enjoyed by the Alpha child. While the natural child may seem too emotional and uninhibited, the Theta child is too inhibited and unemotional. Each child is restricted in part of his own being, less than a total person because of a lack of bilateral consciousness and development. There are those rare individuals who are creative and verbal, who are competent in logic and intuition, who are sensitive and objective, and who are able to perform with competence in both Alpha and Theta behaviors. But usually these individuals excel in spite of our teaching and conditioning; we as teachers can take little credit for their achievements.

The natural child, aside from communication problems with peers, also may take one of several directions in relationship to peers. For example, the highly intuitive and emotional child may feel a great need to share feelings with others, to be liked and admired, and to gain status in the eyes of his peers. Due to his highly sensitive nature and intense emotionality, these natural children appear to constantly surround themselves with

friends; however, they usually end their short friendships pain-
fully as they are unable to maintain their role in the relationship, resulting in their friends leaving the scene in order to be
with more "stable" friends. The natural child may often want
to dominate others. Some natural children are so intense with
their friends that they literally wear them out with endless
minor emotional reactions, disagreements, and fits of temper
and withdrawal when others will not follow their lead. This
egocentric and demanding behavior is seen as not only unfair
and frustrating to their peers, but it causes many children to
exclude the natural child from the group, leaving him alone.

The natural child gets himself in these dilemmas because of
his general ineptness with social values, verbal interaction and
modulation of personal behavior, and a general lack of social
"sense." Classroom games in affective behavior, character education, and the many games involving value clarification are
all important aspects of the natural child's development in
order to counter balance the tendency to avoid social learning.
If it is understood that these children are reaching out for
others without the basic neurological tendencies required in
social learning, then the teacher and parent can empathize with
them and hopefully provide the needed verbal and socialization
structure.

The natural child may take another direction in relation to
peers and this one is as frustrating to parents and teachers as
the emotional response. The second route of development for
the nonverbal creative child is to become so absorbed in his
projects that he simply does not develop the usual social needs
or interest, resulting in behavior that appears at first to be
almost antisocial. The creative world of the Alpha child can be
a totally absorbing experience. One can concentrate all of ones
energies into a particular interest. For example, some children
become hobby "freaks" and spend all of their time with a
specific hobby or interest. Model building, painting, music,
swimming, baseball, or caring for animals all can be examples
of the natural child's unique way of learning which may exclude peers or typical peer interaction. Other children spend
much of their time watching television for the stimulation it

provides in fantasy and visual imagery.

The natural child who truly takes the direction of engaging in activities which satisfy his nonverbal interests may alarm parents and teachers because he simply does not seem interested in peers. One characteristic of these children, aside from their incessant preoccupation with their favorite pastime, is that they tend to select only one friend at a time. If a particular relationship lasts any period of time it is usually because both children tend to be natural children and the basis for their relationship is not that they are friends so much as it is that they share similar interests. It is the interest, the project, or the activity which provides the basis for their interaction. This is to a large degree not so untypical for many children, except that with natural children there is often a lack of the usual emotional and friendship tussles that go on between typically socialized children. If the friend cannot come over on a particular afternoon, they continue on with their project seemingly not disappointed at all that their friends did not join them. This tendency to base a relationship almost totally on a shared absorption in an idea, activity, or project is somewhat unique, not so much because it is different from typical children but because it becomes so exclusively the basis for the relationship.

The natural child who operates on a project-centered relationship often alarms parents and teachers who feel the child is unhappy. It is usually the emotional-creative child mentioned previously who exhibits severe reactions to a lack of friends. The project-centered child seldom seems concerned about friends, and this is as upsetting as the emotional outbursts of the emotional-creative child. Most often the project-centered child will continue in his behavior into adulthood, but it is not particularly a problem. Most children only need one friend at a time to learn most of the personal and social skills required for an adult life which will be somewhat reclusive and certainly project- or work-centered rather than people-centered. It is not so much a problem as simply another way to be. It is usually the verbal and social parents and teachers who feel upset for these children because they do not understand, from their own reference point, how anyone could be happy without the typical level of social interaction. An appropriate response to their concern might be that the Alpha child does not understand how they could be happy being around so many people so much of the time.

These general suggestions provide at least an overview of some of the traits of the natural child, traits which may be viewed by others as "problems." If these "problems" can be understood as unique to the Alpha child's nature and included in the range of normal behavioral possibilities, then these children will not end up labeled as learning disabled, emotionally disturbed, or socially deviant.

REFERENCES

1. Ayres, A.: *Sensory Integration and Learning Disorders.* Los Angeles, Western Psychological Services, 1972.
2. Geschwind, N. and Levitsky, W.: Human brain: left-right asymmetries in temporal speech region. *Science, 161*:186-187, 1968.
3. Teszner, D.: Anatomical Studies of the Right-Left Asymmetry of the Temporal Plane on the Heads of One Hundred Adults. Doctoral Thesis, University of Paris, 1972.
4. Bakwin, H. and Bakwin, R. M.: *Clinical Management of Behavioral Disorders in Children.* Philadelphia, Saunders, 1966.
5. Werry, J. S.: Developmental hyperactivity. *Pediatr Clin North Am, 15*:581-599, 1968.
6. Hutt, C., Hutt, S. J., and Ounsted, C.: The behavior of children with and without upper central nervous system lesions. *Behavior, 24*:246-248, 1965.
7. Ounsted, C., Lindsay, J., and Norman R.: Biological factors in temporal lobe epilepsy. In *Clinics in Developmental Medicine,* No. 22. London, Heinemann, 1965.
8. Laufer, M. W., Denhoff, E., and Solomons, G.: Hyperkinetic impulse disorders in children's behavior problems. *Psychosomatic Med, 19:38-49,* 1957.
9. Weiss, G., Minde, K., Werry, J. S., Douglas, V., and Nemeth, E.: Studies on the hyperactive child, VIII; five year followup. *Arch Gen Psychiatry, 24*:409-414, 1971.
10. Piaget, J.: *The Origins of Intelligence in Children.* Trans by M. Cook. New York, Int Univ Pr, 1952.
11. Kephart, N. C.: *The Slow Learner in the Classroom.* Columbus, Ohio, Merrill, 1960.
12. Markoff, A. M.: *Teaching Low Achieving Children Reading, Spelling, and Handwriting.* Springfield, Thomas, 1976.

BIBLIOGRAPHY

Ayres, A. J.: *Sensory Integration and Learning*. Los Angeles, Western Psych, 1972.

Bakan, P.: The eyes have it. *Psychology Today, 4(11)*:64-97, April, 1971.

Bakwin, H. and Bakwin, R. M.: *Clinical Management of Behavioral Disorders in Children*. Philadelphia, Saunders, 1966.

Bloom, B. et al.: *Taxonomy of Educational Objectives: The Classification of Educational Goals, Handbook II, Affective Domain*. New York, McKay, 1956.

Bogen, J. E. and Bogen, G. M.: The other side of the brain, III, the corpus callosum and creativity. *Bull Los Angeles Neurol Soc, 34*:191-220, 1969.

Dimond, S. J.: Hemisphere function and word registration. *J Exp Psychol, 87*:183-186, 1971.

Dimond, S. J. and Beaumont, J. C.: The use of two hemispheres to increase brain capacity. *Nature, 232*:270-271, 1971.

——— Processing in perceptual integration between and within the cerebral hemispheres. *Br J Psychol, 63*:509-514, 1972.

——— Different personality patterns of human cerebral hemispheres. In press.

——— *Hemisphere Function in the Human Brain*. New York, Wiley, 1974.

Ferinden, W. Jr., and Jackson, S.: *Educational Interpretation of the Wechsler Intelligence Scale for Children*. Linden, NJ, Remediation Associates, 1969.

Gazzaniga, M. S., Bogen, J. E., and Sperry, R. W.: Dyspraxia following division of the cerebral commissures. *Arch Neurol, 16*:606-612, 1967.

Geschwind, N. and Levitsky, W.: Human brain: left-right asymmetries in temporal speech region. *Science, 161*:186-187, 1968.

Hebb, D. O.: *Introduction to Psychology*. Philadelphia, Saunders, 1966.

Hunter, M.: Right brained kids in left brained schools. *Today's Education, 65*:45-48, Nov-Dec 1976.

Hutt, C., Hutt, S. J., and Ounsted: The behavior of children with and without upper central nervous system lesions. *Behavior, 24*:246-248, 1965.

Kephart, N. C.: *The Slow Learner in the Classroom*. Columbus, Ohio, Merrill, 1960.

Laufer, M. W., Denhoff, E., and Solomons, G.: Hyperkinetic impulse disorders in children's behavior problems. *Psychosom Med, 19*:38-49, 1957.

Levy-Agresti, J. and Sperry, R. W.: Differential perceptual capabilities in

229

major and minor hemispheres. *Proc Natl Acad Sci USA, 61*:1151, 1968.

Levy-Agresti, J. and Trevarthen, C.: Perceptual, sematic, and phonetic aspects of elementary language processes in split-brain patients. *Brain, 100*:105-108, 1977.

Markoff, A. M.: *Teaching Low Achieving Children Reading, Spelling and Handwriting.* Springfield, Thomas, 1976.

Ornstein, R. E.: *The Psychology of Consciousness.* New York, Grossman, 1976.

———— *Mind Field.* New York, Grossman, 1976.

Ounsted, C., Lindsay, J., and Norman, R.: Biological factors in temporal lobe epilepsy. In *Clinics in Developmental Medicine,* No. 22. London, Heinemann, 1965.

Penfield, W.: *The Mystery of the Mind: a critical study of consciousness and the human brain.* Princeton NJ, Princeton U Pr, 1975.

Piaget, J.: *The Origins of Intelligence in Children.* Trans. by M. Cook. New York, Intl Univs Pr, 1952.

Sage, W.: The Split brain lab. *Human Behavior, 5*:24, June, 1976.

Sperry, R. W.: A modified concept of consciousness. *Psychol Rev, 76*:532-536, 1969.

Teszner, D.: Anatomical Studies of the Right-Left Asymmetry of the Temporal Plane on the Heads of One Hundred Adults. Doctoral thesis, U Paris, 1972.

Weiss, G. et al.: Studies on the hyperactive child, five-year followup. *Arch Gen Psychiatry, 24*:409-414, 1971.

Werry, J. S.: Developmental hyperactivity. *Pediatr Clin North Am, 15*:581-599, 1968.

Yahraes, H.: *Detection and Prevention of Learning Disorders.* Rockville, MD, National Institute of Mental Health, 1976.

INDEX

231